EVERYWHERE I LOOK
GOD IS THERE

EVERYWHERE I LOOK
GOD IS THERE

180 Daily Devotional Discoveries

Susan Roberts

CLADACH
Publishing

Published by CLADACH Publishing
PO Box 336144 Greeley, CO 80633
http://cladach.com

Cover photo: iStock/©LightingKreative

Library of Congress Control Number: 2016958387

ISBN-13: 9781945099007
ISBN-10: 1945099003

Printed in the United States of America

Dedicated to:

First of all, my awesome God who has inspired and guided in this process. He truly showed up every day. I offer this to Him to use for His purposes in encouraging, motivating, convicting and inspiring readers, as they develop their relationships with Him. May all be to His honor and glory.

Secondly, my incredible husband, Perry. He knew I could do it. He has been at my side the whole way, photographing, proofing, encouraging, helping, making calls, gathering information—my goodness, what has he not done? I am so grateful for him, his love and his support! Thanks, Perry! I love you!

TABLE OF CONTENTS

INTRODUCTION

The trek across the rock-strewn beach with its sharp and slippery terrain is rough going. Yet this is a favorite activity—not because I relish the hard walk, but because of the anticipated treasures. I find rocks at the water's edge and turn them over to see what I can find. It takes a bit of effort, but with a sucking sound, a rock will finally move, opening a puddle-filled depression that is often home to a host of critters. This causes yells of, "Com'ere and look at this!"

Sometimes our trek in life is rough going. We wish our walk took us over smooth sand instead of rocks and bumps. But in those very difficulties we often uncover treasures from God: his goodness, his love, his faithfulness, and his strength. We often focus on the hard steps we have to make and become discouraged. But if we would stop and look with anticipation, we would see: God is there. And he is eager to reveal himself to us. God has promised that if we seek him, we will find him (*see* Jeremiah 29:13).

My spiritual, seeking journey started quite unexpectedly. I was praying, asking God where he wanted me to serve. The word "write" kept coming to mind. "I hear you God, but write what?" I had no clue what he meant.

Two years later, as a new parishioner in a local church, my husband and I were sitting in the pastor's office discussing our grandson's upcoming baptism service. Out of the blue, our pastor changed the subject and told us that the woman who did the church prayer line had fallen and broken her hip. She could no longer do this ministry. Then the pastor asked if I would be interested. Skeptical, I inquired about what it entailed. "Compiling incoming prayer requests two or three times a week for emails and a phone line, and writing a devotional." Yes! This was what God was calling me to do.

Thus began an incredible journey. At first, writing devotions was easy. I had lots of ideas. It didn't take long to get to the point where I came up dry. On prayer line mornings, I would pray for God to give me an idea, and he always showed up. He began revealing himself and his truth to me in the most unlikely of places all the time—not just on prayer-line days. Now, after six years, I can say, "Everywhere I look, God is there."

God will show up for you, too—maybe not in the same ways he does for me—but you can count on him. Just look. He is there.

WINTER

PHOTO © Susan Roberts

FROZEN

A cold front roared in, bringing sub-freezing weather. I usually leave a water bottle in my car so I can sip as I go, but today I was disappointed. My water bottle had frozen as hard as a rock. I knew if I waited awhile, the warmth of the car would at least partially melt the ice so I could somewhat quench my thirst. What a relief to finally get a drink of that cold water. I think the longing had increased my thirst.

God's promises are sometimes like that. I see them, I know they are there and that they are good and helpful, but they seem frozen in God's timing. My need and situation make it very hard to wait. I want them, and I want them now. It would even be nice if I knew God's answer would be available in an hour or two, a day, a week, or even a month. Then I could endure.

God is not like that. his timing is a mystery. Job certainly experienced unbelievable difficulty, yet he still trusted God. God wants our faith and trust in spite of circumstances. He will act in the best way at the right time. He will pour out his Spirit. We need to wait for him. In the meantime, we can strengthen our faith by immersing ourselves in God's Word. Then, wait patiently for the Lord, however long it takes, persevering, and not losing hope. His refreshing drink of living water is coming.

"Hope that is seen is no hope at all. Who hopes for what they already have? But if we hope for what we do not yet have, we wait for it patiently." (Romans 8:24-25)

PHOTO © Arnold Wheat

TO CANCEL OR NOT TO CANCEL

To cancel or not to cancel: that is the question. Whenever a major snowstorm is imminent, officials have to decide whether or not to close schools and businesses. They try to get the most updated weather forecasts, looking at maps and meteorologists' projections. Road crews and the highway patrol are queried about conditions. District authorities collaborate. They consider the impact on the safety of students and drivers, and the inconveniences to parents, workers and the community.

Our neighbor was once faced with the decision of shutting down the Denver Mint in a snowstorm. It had never closed before. his boss was out of town and he was in charge. He struggled with making this historic decision, but after lots of input, he felt he made a wise choice to close the doors.

We all face frequent decisions, though they might not have the far-reaching impact of school and business closures. Sometimes we make choices on the spur of the moment or with "gut" feelings. At other times, we seek advice from trusted friends or professionals. It is wise not to "go it alone." Solomon, in his wisdom, wrote that seeking counsel helps plans succeed (see Proverbs 15:22, 20:18). The best counsel we can receive, however, is from the Lord, who can truly see the big picture—all the facets, impacts, and even the future. Are you facing decisions? Don't go it alone.

"For this God is our God forever and ever; He will be our guide even to the end."
(Psalm 48:14)

PHOTO © Dr. John Dennehy

JUGGLING

The Guinness Book of World Records includes five pages of juggling records. Jugglers use torches, balls, rings, plates, clubs, even chain saws. Alex Barron currently holds the record for the most balls juggled. The competition is fierce. There is underwater juggling, upside down juggling, juggling while skiing, snowboarding or jumping on a pogo stick, and joggling over hurdles. Endurance feats are listed—can you juggle a soccer ball with your foot for twenty-four hours straight, or run a 5K while juggling? 524 people in Baltimore simultaneously juggled 1,997 objects! Bob Nickerson is noted for dribbling four basketballs simultaneously and for juggling three basketballs while shooting twenty-five consecutive lay-ups!

Today I felt like a world-class juggler. I barely had time to breathe: phone ringing, people stopping by, fax machine humming, emails coming, projects due, deadlines looming. Under such stress it is easy to snap at people and be less than courteous, especially when someone asks a dumb question for the third time. I found myself praying for focus and calm. Scriptures came to mind: "Whatever your hand finds to do, do it with your might" (Ecclesiastes 9:10) and "Live a life worthy of the Lord, pleasing him in every way" (Colossians 1:10-11). We are blessed to have a heavenly Father who hears our prayers and is there with grace to help in time of need. If your week gets hectic with too much to do, rest in the Lord and remember:

"I can do all things through Christ who gives me strength!" (Philippians 4:13)

PHOTO © CanStockPhoto Inc / JanDix

FINDING A HEART

One morning when I arrived at work, I found a small heart-shaped necklace on my desk. Apparently the custodians found it over the weekend and set it out of the way. It was inscribed with a single word: "love." What a wonderful way to kick-off the week! I took this love message as **a reminder**:

- **that I am loved**. What an awesome God we have who loves us just as we are in spite of ourselves and wants to take care of us, give us good gifts and enter into a relationship with us.

- **to love those around me**. It is important for me to act with love and kindness, and put myself in others' shoes, feeling their fear and frustration, then lovingly helping them cope. All around me, people need a kind word or smile, a helping hand and a thoughtful act. As I have come to realize the magnitude of God's love for me, I'm able to love myself and let that love overflow to others. What about those who are hard to love? C.S. Lewis wrote, "Do not waste time bothering whether you 'love' your neighbor; act as if you did.…When you are behaving as if you loved someone you will presently come to love him."[1]

"Dear friends, let us love one another, for love is of God. Everyone who loves has been born of God and knows God." (1 John 4:7-8, NIVUK)

1. Quoted from C.S. Lewis, *Mere Christianity* by CS Lewis (Macmillan, 1952).

PHOTO © CanStockPhoto Inc / AnnieAnnie

TRASH PICK UP

The rumble and grind in the street reminded us that it was "trash pick-up day." Trash trucks were out and about; sanitation workers diligently removed all the refuse. We are grateful for our trash service—they take away almost anything (within reason), in nearly any form. We can "clean house" and rely on them to get rid of all our unwanted stuff and garbage.

When we lived in Washington, we were not as fortunate. If our one allowed garbage can wasn't secured with a tightly closed lid, they would not pick it up. Additional cans were very expensive. In the Chicago area, we were allowed two cans (also tightly closed), but any yard waste had to be disposed of in special biodegradable bags purchased from the city at over a dollar each. Nothing outside of a can or a bag would be removed. It was a challenge to dispose of unwanted garbage.

Isn't it great that God picks up and gets rid of whatever we agree to throw out? He doesn't set limits or refuse certain items. He forgives us and removes all our transgressions. Let's set a "Trash day" and get rid of the things that keep us from doing God's work effectively.

> "In a large house there are articles not only of gold and silver, but also of wood and clay; some are for special purposes and some for common use. Those who cleanse themselves from the latter will be instruments for special purposes, made holy, useful to the Master and prepared to do any good work." (2 Timothy 2:20-21, NIVUK)

PHOTO © CanStockPhoto Inc / ingridhs

HANDLING GOD'S TRUTH

"Truth? You can't handle the truth!" You may recognize this quote from the movie "A Few Good Men" starring Tom Cruise and Jack Nicholson. Watching this movie recently, I thought: *Sometimes the truth's reality is difficult to face.*

Our society can't handle the truth—God's truth, that is. his truth is absolute. He has catalogued it in his Word. He says there is one way only.

We need to be bold and speak God's truth in a generation that has lost sight of what truth really is. This requires taking risks. People will not like it. They will think we are intolerant, prejudiced and unaccepting of diversity. Yet, it must be done. We must stand firm on God's Word and not waiver when the going gets tough. Our voice must be heard. We are on the brink of the last days. Our country hangs in the balance and has been found wanting.

Let us work to clean up our own lives, and then through the power of prayer, speak the Word of the Lord boldly with his wisdom and guidance. Who knows? Revival may sweep across this country. I love this country. I'm sad to see it falter. Are you? Let us begin this year praying for God to heal and bless America, as we rise to serve him and speak his truth.

It really starts with each of us. We must learn and adhere to God's truth, confessing our own sin, and humbling ourselves before Almighty God so he can use us in mighty ways.

"If my people who are called by my name, will humble themselves and pray and seek my face and turn from their wicked ways, then I will hear and will forgive their sin and heal their land." (2 Chronicles 7:14)

PHOTOS © Larry Lawton

CHOSEN

Throughout the tropical garden colorful butterflies flitted among the flowers and waterfalls, landing on plants, rocks and even on visitors. We had taken some time during the holidays to visit the Butterfly Pavilion in Westminster, Colorado with our kids and grandkids. The pavilion is home to over 5,000 animals and has a variety of insects as well as sea creatures in their aquarium. But the main attraction is the butterflies. If you wear bright colored clothing, chances are a wee winged creature will land on you. As we headed to the garden, we stopped to hold Rosie, the tarantula, admire the walking sticks (insects) and gasp at the icky roaches. We played on the zip line and rope ladder. Then we headed into the butterfly room. We all enjoyed—or so I thought—the walk on winding paths as beautiful, colorful butterflies surrounded us. When we got back in the car, my grandson was very quiet. "Why the long face?" I asked. "Didn't you have a good time?" He was disappointed that a butterfly had not chosen to land on him.

We later thought, how wonderful it is that God has chosen to "land on us," bringing his love, redemption and grace! What an awesome truth to consider during the Christmas season as we celebrate Jesus' coming to us. This should bring a smile to your face!

"But you are a chosen people, a royal priesthood, a holy nation, a people belonging to God, that you may declare the praises of him who called you out of darkness into his wonderful light." (1 Peter 2:9)

PHOTO © Susan Roberts

TRANSFORMER

The warehouse doors opened and out stepped a huge metallic creature that was over one story tall. Kids, waiting in line for pictures, squealed in delight. We were at Universal Studios' Transformer show. Prior to the presentation, the monsters mingled with the crowd. Once inside, we witnessed these huge creatures changing from ordinary cars, trucks and planes to monstrous crime-fighting machines in only a moment, ready to take on the challenges that came their way.

Wouldn't it be great if we too could change our ways and habits instantly, and be empowered to fight the good fight? When we become Christ followers, we become "a new creation" (*see* 2 Corinthians 5:17). But somewhere along the line, like the transformers who change back to the ordinary, we can lose our focus and resolve and slip back to our old, ineffective, sinful selves. So, what's the strategy to remain strong? Romans 12:2 tells us not to be conformed to the world, but transformed into the person God intended us to be. We do this by renewing our minds and developing a God focus rather than world focus. We also have an incredible power source. The Lord gives us strength as we wait on him. God's strength is perfected even in our weaknesses. Let's not be "transformers," but be transformed through God's Spirit in us.

"Do not conform any longer to the pattern of this world, but be transformed by the renewing of your mind. Then you will be able to test and approve what God's will is—his good, pleasing and perfect will." (Romans 12:2)

PHOTO © CanStockPhoto Inc / Madhourse

STARS

Have you ever taken a telescope and pointed it at the stars? It's an amazing sight as previously-invisible stars appear out of the blackness. Observatories with their powerful lenses reveal even more. Air and light pollution limit even the most powerful telescopes, though. We witnessed the difference pollution makes when we visited Arches National Park in Utah. The sky was a blanket of stars, with hardly any empty space. The dry air and remote location make this one of the best star-gazing sites in America.

With the Hubble Space Telescope's powerful lens, humans can see farther than ever before. It is positioned in space where it can photograph remote stars, planets, and galaxies, reachings far beyond our earthly perspective.

Our earthly perspective, tainted by the worldly pollution of sin, self-centeredness, worry and distraction, makes it difficult for us to look heaven-ward. God tells us that he is our high tower (*see* 2 Samuel 22:3). We can go to him to rise above the darkness and to see his light more clearly. We can gaze at his bright truth and promises, rather than our earthly troubles. Jesus came to teach us about God and reveal the mysteries of his truth and life. His powerful lens sharpens our image of God so that we can know him, his purposes and amazing love and care for us. We do not need to be earthbound when we are heaven bound. Look up and see.

> "When I consider your heavens, the work of your fingers, the moon and stars, which you have set in place, what is man that you are mindful of him, the son of man that you care for him?" (Psalm 8:3-4)

PHOTO © CanStockPhoto Inc / Gregor_Scholl

MISTLETOE

While visiting friends in Texas, I was excited to see mistletoe growing in the trees. I even took a knife and cut some to bring home for our Christmas decorating. Our friends were not excited about mistletoe. It is a parasite that saps food and nutrients from the tree, stunting its growth and commonly killing the branch where it is growing. A heavy infestation may kill the whole tree. It spreads quickly and is very difficult to destroy.

Worry is like mistletoe. Many of us take worries upon ourselves, but they sap our strength and can destroy our attitude, enthusiasm, rest, and health. Worry obscures God's light and truth, and can be very difficult to overcome.

We may have concern about many things, but concern is different from worry. Concern stimulates action towards a solution, while worry is counter-productive. We do not need to avoid difficulties, sticking our heads in the sand, and not dealing with the problems, hoping they'll just go away. We do need to approach problems responsibly. Worry is not the answer. Our anxiety cannot change the situation, or get us through. But, God can. Scripture tells us not to worry, but to trust God in everything (*see* Matthew 6:25-34). When we take our concerns to Jesus, he can guide us to act in wise ways and give us peace while he works things out for our good.

"Therefore, I tell you, do not worry about your life...who of you by worrying can add a single hour to his life? Your heavenly Father knows what you need. Seek first his kingdom and his righteousness and all these things will be given to you as well."
(Matthew 6:25-34)

PHOTO © Dr. Ed Holroyd

BLACK SWANS

Beautiful white swans have inspired songs, poems, and stories. Up until 1697, when the Dutch explorer Willem de Vlamingh discovered black swans in Western Australia[2], only white swans were presumed to exist. A common expression in 16th-century London refered to an utter impossibility as a black swan. Black swans are still used as a metaphor for something that is highly unlikely or nearly impossible, something that has shocking and life-changing impact.

I was privileged to hear John-Michael Keyes, father of Emily Keyes, who was killed in a school shooting at Platte Canyon High School. In his presentation he referred to the horrific event as a black swan. John has taken this horrible tragedy and turned it into something very positive. He said Emily's last gift to him was "a voice." He has set up a foundation to work on school safety from district to national levels. The biggest hurdle he faces is the false security of folks who think, "This could never happen to me."

John Michael explained that peace comes not from the absence of stress or worry, nor from denial. Peace is the calm in our hearts in the midst of it all. As Christian believers, we do not have to be consumed by events outside our control. We know that God will be with us in all things. Let him quiet your heart and give the strength to move on and make a difference.

"Peace I leave with you; my peace I give you. I do not give to you as the world gives. Do not let your heart be troubled and do not be afraid." (John 14:27)

2. *The Origin of Life on Perth 1697*, ©2007 by LifeOnPerth.com

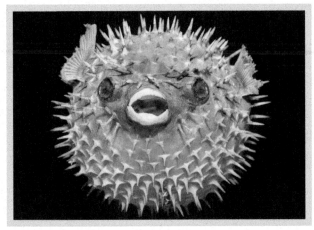

PHOTO © CanStockPhoto Inc / kostya6969

PUFFERFISH

In tropical oceans there lives an unobtrusive fish called a Pufferfish. Most of the time, this creature hides or clumsily scavenges along the ocean floor. When threatened, however, it quickly inflates with water or air to several times its normal size. In addition, hidden spines filled with a deadly poison appear and ward off predators. In spite of its small size, this is quite an intimidating fish!

We also employ defense mechanisms when we feel threatened. Sometimes we hide and do not wish others to see us as we really are. At other times we might puff ourselves up to appear greater or more spiritual than we really are, to impress others (*see* Romans 12:3). Sometimes we lash out at others with unkind words, gossip or judgments that can have a poisonous effect, in the hope that making them appear small will elevate our own stature.

One of the great things about God's grace is that he accepts us as we are. We don't need to make ourselves into something we are not to earn his favor. We don't need to hide in fear. As we learn to accept God's grace, we can learn to accept ourselves. That in turn lowers our defenses so we can love others more. We no longer need to put on airs to impress, or use poisonous barbs to put someone in their place.

As we bask in the knowledge of God's unconditional love and amazing grace, we can also seek to love others as we are loved.

"Love suffers long and is kind; love does not envy; love does not parade itself, is not puffed up." (1 Corinthians 13: 4, NKJV)

PHOTO © CanStockPhoto Inc / Chretien

FOOTPRINTS

Freshly fallen snow is beautiful. It blankets the ground and all imperfections disappear. I can no longer see the unpulled weeds, the unraked leaves, the bare spots in the lawn and the cracks in the sidewalk. It is especially fun to see the footprints where wild critters have walked and wonder "Who goes there and what are you up to?" When the snow melts, however, the prints disappear and imperfections show themselves again.

In the Psalms, David says that God covers our iniquities (*see* Psalms 32:1) like the blanket of snow covers my yard. Our sin is covered up. Unseeable. However, this is not temporary, with our sins showing up again now and then. We don't have to worry about the past, thinking our sins will come back to require more attention. All we have to do is confess our sins, knowing that God is faithful and just to forgive them. He will cleanse us from all unrighteousness (*see* 1 John 1:9). When our sins are covered by God's blanket of snow, we are also reconciled to him and can enter into a relationship with him. We then begin to notice the footprints of his activity in our lives. his Spirit is at work in and through us always, even when we don't see him. Let us thank God for his all-covering forgiveness, and his faithful work in our lives!

"'Come now, let us reason together,' says the Lord. 'Though your sins are like scarlet, they shall be as white as snow; though they are red as crimson, they shall be like wool.'" (Isaiah 1:18)

PHOTO © Dr. Ed Holroyd

SNOWFLAKES

I find snowflake fascinating. There are many different kinds and shapes. Warmer temperatures produce something more like a ball than a flake, similar to hail. The best snowflakes come when there are very cold temperatures and winds. Water molecules, high in the clouds, freeze and form six-sided crystals. As they swirl around in the wind currents, they pass through different temperature zones, producing varying rates of growth. The most beautiful snowflakes occur when the temperature is between 3-10° F. Then each side forms sharp points that branch out into intricate, unique patterns. The longer the flakes are airborne, the more time they have to develop their form. Since each one takes a different route and spends varying time aloft, no two are exactly alike. Not all of them, however, are symmetrical. Dust particles on the snowflake slow the crystal's development and a lopsided snowflake results.[3]

We are much like snowflakes! God has formed each one of us to be unique and has laid out different paths for us to walk. The more we are buffeted by adverse conditions of life, the more beautiful and multi-faceted we can become. We need those tough times to fully develop into what God intended us to be. Yes, the dirt of sin can retard our growth; but God is still in the business of making us beautiful. He works even through the bad situations to bring about the best for us.

"We know that all that happens to us is working for our good if we love God and are fitting into his plans." (Romans 8:28, TLB)

3. "Snowflake Chemistry—Answers to Common Questions" (Accessed at http://chemistry.about.com/od/moleculescompounds/a/snowflake.htm on 10-25-2016).

PHOTO © Jana Osterlund

OVER THE MOUNTAINS

We have a beautiful view of the mountains from our kitchen nook. As I stand and pray in front of the window, I am reminded of David's Psalm 121: "I lift up my eyes to the mountains—where does my help come from? My help comes from the Lord, the Maker of heaven and earth." I envision King David, praying by his window, looking out and imagining God's power and majesty pouring in on the clouds over the mountains.

The mountains, to me, have also become a symbol of God's ever-present help. This morning they were pretty hazy after the storms of the past couple of days, and seemed far away. Yesterday, in fact, we could not see them at all. Some days, however, they are crystal clear and seem almost close enough to reach out and touch.

That is indicative of the way I perceive God's help. Sometimes his work is very evident and clear. Other times, it seems far away and murky. Sometimes I cannot see it at all. But just like the mountains, it has not changed or moved. Only my perception has changed. In spite of our circumstances, God wants our faith and trust, because he is faithful and trustworthy!

> "He will not let your foot slip—he who watches over you will not slumber; indeed, he who watches over Israel will neither slumber nor sleep. The Lord watches over you—the Lord is your shade at your right hand; the sun will not harm you by day, nor the moon by night. The Lord will keep you from all harm—he will watch over your life; the Lord will watch over your coming and going both now and forevermore." (Psalm 121:1-8)

PHOTO © CanStockPhoto Inc / sandsphoto

DECORAH EAGLES

Beginning in February, the Decorah Eagle cam posts live video feed of an eagle nest in Decorah, Iowa. It can be viewed online. There you can watch these eagles sit on their eggs and then care for the young. The mother and father take turns. The camera stays on the eagles until the eaglets hatch and fly away. Success! We saw one eagle covered in snow, sitting faithfully on the nest. It reminded me of the Dr. Seuss book, *Horton Hatches An Egg,* where the elephant sits on the nest through all kinds of weather and utters that famous line: "An elephant's faithful 100%!"

We are so blessed to have a 100% faithful God who will never leave us! "He will cover you with his feathers, and under his wings you will find refuge; his faithfulness will be your shield and rampart" (Psalm 91:4). "Because of the Lord's great love we are not consumed, for his compassions never fail. They are new every morning; great is your faithfulness" (Lamentations 3:22-24).

We too are called to be faithful. "Let love and faithfulness never leave you; bind them around your neck, write them on the tablet of your heart. Then you will win favor and a good name in the sight of God and man (Proverbs 3:3-4). We have the help of God's people and God's Spirit. Through thick and thin, and all kinds of weather, let us endeavor to be God's faithful workers, so that when our time on earth is over, God may say:

"Well done, good and faithful servant!" (Matthew 25:21)

PHOTO © Dr. John Dennehy

SNOW ANGELS

The snow was falling. As we headed to bed, our deck and lawn were already covered with an inch of snow. Early the next morning, in childlike anticipation, I peeked out of the window to see how much snow had fallen. The trees and shrubs, weighted down with garbs of white, appeared somewhat surreal in the shadows of the streetlights, but the street, thankfully, was clear.

I like the snow. I remember the childhood anticipation of a day off from school. I have fond memories of childhood snowball fights, snowman building, angel making, and sledding. However, adult responsibilities and concerns have now taken their toll. Driving in the stuff is no fun, and I dislike the impediment to plans. Still, I peek out the window with a sense of exhilaration.

God wants us to approach him with childlike faith and anticipation. Our adult practicality gets in the way. We become cynical and lose our sense of fun and wonder. We feel the weight of responsibilities. It doesn't have to be that way. The Spirit can increase our joy and faith so that we relish life, seeing God at work all around us. We can eagerly anticipate evidence of his awesome power as we wait on him. He is willing to take on our burdens so that our hearts can be light. In the Gospels we read that Jesus called a little child to his side and had him stand in the middle of them all. He presented this child as an example of trust, faith, and joy. Let us find our inner child and respond to God with wide-eyed faith, unabashed joy, and eager anticipation. We will be amazed at what he will do.

"Unless you change and become like little children, you will never enter the kingdom of heaven." (Matthew 18:2-4)

PHOTO © Susan Roberts

CONTAINER GARDENING

This photo doesn't look like winter! Even now, though, I'm getting ready for spring planting. A few years ago, because of our poor soil, I decided to switch from garden beds to containers. It was fun designing the layout, making paths between the boxes and building the sprinkler system. After all was done, there was a sense of accomplishment, joy and pride. Now it requires care, which I provide with enthusiasm. I took advantage of a balmy winter day to repair some broken sprinkler heads, clean out some debris and condition the soil. I've also been drawing plans of planting, and poring through seed catalogues to order what I'll need.

When God created the world, he relished each task and saw that it was good (see Genesis 1:31). It has been said that constructing something engages only the hands while creating something engages the heart. I believe God truly put his heart into what he made because he loves us and wanted to do something awesome for us to enjoy. When God created people, he made us to be something special, in his image, with a desire to create and a free will to choose. But humankind rebelled and became broken. God set about caring for us and repairing us with the same resolve, love and joy with which he created the world. In his love for us, he sent Jesus. his sacrifice on the cross reconciled us to God, repaired our brokenness, and gave us newness of life. He is now carrying out his plan.

"Therefore, if anyone is in Christ, he is a new creation." (2 Corinthians 5:17a)

PHOTO © Jeff Osterlund

YANKING OUT WEEDS

It's that time of year—out with the old, in with the new. We probably all have stuff we'd like to get rid of—like weeds. Yank 'em out and start fresh. But yanking out weeds will not necessarily get rid of them. Often, a bit of root or seed can grow again. And the empty holes invite other weeds to take up residence. If you have some yanking to do, make sure you get to the root.

Between you and God, what is holding you back? Confess your sin and ask God to help you get rid of that destructive behavior which has rooted itself in your spirit, preventing good things from growing (*see* Hebrews 12:15). Then, use weed mat. God's love and grace covers a multitude of sin. Accept God's forgiveness. Cover yourself with his love (*see* Romans 4:7-8). Rest under the shadow of his protection (*see* Psalm 91:1). Finally, plant new stuff. The Holy Spirit can fill you with his power, truth and fruit.

Though it's freezing out, and not especially the time to think of gardening, we can start the new year by planting a spiritual garden that brings honor and glory to God. The Great Gardener of the universe waits to give us a hand.

> "I pray that out of his glorious riches he may strengthen you with power through his Spirit in your inner being, so that Christ may dwell in your hearts through faith....that you, being rooted and established in love, may have power, together with all the Lord's holy people, to grasp how wide and long and high and deep is the love of Christ, and to know this love that surpasses knowledge—that you may be filled to the measure of all the fullness of God." (Ephesians 3:16-19)

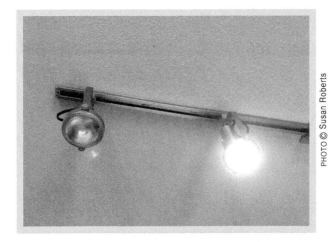

PHOTO © Susan Roberts

BURNOUT

A light bulb burned out in our closet, and we had to fumble around in the dark. As short as I am, it was challenging to try and change it. I decided it was worth the hassle, though, to have light again.

About that time our son, a youth pastor, visited. We discussed the topic of ministry burnout. Ministers sometimes burn out and need a change after a few years. But others experience this as well. Those caring for a senior parent or a young child can experience compassion fatigue. A mundane or demanding job may cause burnout. Dealing with an illness with endless procedures and trips to the doctor can be overwhelming. Even volunteers can burn out if they feel their task is thankless, unimportant, and ineffective. It may be time for a change; but change is not always an option.

In our house, we have several appliances that run down but can be recharged. We have flashlights, computers, a sweeper and cell phones that need to be plugged in periodically to provide renewed power and light. This is another strategy for burn out. We all need to take time to recharge. Follow the example God set for us when he rested after creation. Jesus also took time out from his ministry to get away from the crowds and pray. It might be a stretch to find that time, but we must make ourselves rest so that we will be refreshed with the needed power and light from God.

Let us seek God's wisdom to discern if change or rest is what we need to continue in effectiveness.

"There remains then, a Sabbath rest for the people of God." (Hebrews 4: 9-10)

PHOTO © Susan Roberts

CROCK POT

Looking forward to a delicious meal, I got out my favorite slow-cooker recipe. Even though I was in a hurry, I followed the recipe precisely. I plopped the roast into the crock pot, dumped in the spices and water, added potatoes and carrots, secured the lid, and turned the dial to high. Then I hustled out the door. One important step was overlooked. I came home to a raw, cold, inedible chunk of meat. I had not plugged in the pot! What a big disappointment. My husband and I had to make other dinner plans.

We, as Christians are not very palatable, either, unless we are "plugged in" to God. We can have all the right ingredients for a successful Christian life: church attendance, Bible studies, prayer meetings, community service—but we just aren't that effective without God's power. We need another plan. God wants us to remain connected to him and abide with him in a personal way so He can bring us to "doneness"—his completed work in us (*see* Philippians1:6). We get connected by making contact with him—reading his Word, praising and praying. Then we can be fruitful and effective as his power works in us. We really cannot do anything without him (*see* John 15:5). We have this same responsibility. There are a lot of hungry people out there who need Jesus to satisfy their innermost needs. Don't remain raw, cold, and indifferent. Are you ready to serve? Get plugged in.

"Feed my sheep." (John 21:15)

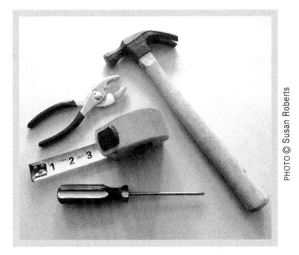

PHOTO © Susan Roberts

TOOLS

Have you ever improvised when you didn't have the right tool? I've pounded in nails with a shoe and cut an apple with a nail file. My husband has opened bottles with his teeth. Whether in the kitchen or workshop, it is best to have the right tool for the job. I wouldn't flip a pancake with a spoon or tighten a bolt with a tape measure. Who would level a line with a hammer or remove a screw with a wrench?

Each of us are a special tool in God's tool box, created with specific gifts, talents, and purpose. Are you trying to do someone else's job even though it doesn't fit your calling? Do you think you have to do it all? When a few of us busy bees take over everything, we are denying someone else the chance to use their gifts and serve. Back off. If a door is open, maybe the person who should be stepping up to the plate will be motivated to help out. They may have been reluctant because they didn't feel wanted and thought everything was covered. Each of us, as members of the body of Christ, should be fulfilling our specific role. We are not all hands or feet, and an eye cannot do what an ear does.

"But in fact God has arranged the parts in the body, every one of them, just as he wanted them to be....Now you are the body of Christ, and each one of you is a part of it." (1 Corinthians 12:18, 27)

PHOTO © Susan Roberts

FOLLOWING THE RECIPE

In my hurried holiday baking, I sometimes don't follow recipes precisely. When I'm improvising or inattentive, the results can be undesirable.

As I read the Christmas story in Matthew, I discovered another group that had trouble following recipes. John the Baptist was given the task of preparing the way for the Lord. The Sadducees and Pharisees wouldn't follow God's simple plan to repent and believe. They were caught up in their own recipe for righteousness. It was not successful. They resisted when John tried to show them the right way. When Jesus began his ministry, they wouldn't listen to him either. They refused to follow God's way and relied on their own initiatives instead. They had all the appropriate information from the prophets, but they didn't pay attention.

God's message to us today is simple too: Repent and believe in his Son. It is all about his grace. We cannot follow a different recipe to earn God's favor, have a fulfilling life or gain entrance into heaven. We cannot be inattentive to his Word. We cannot rely on our good works and best efforts. We cannot even rely on others. To be victorious in this life we need to carefully follow God's plan of salvation by believing in Jesus alone. Nothing else. Jesus came so that we could have life, that we could be reconciled to God and that we could be victorious over sin and death. Trust him and his plan.

"I am the way, the truth and the life. No one comes to the Father except through me." (John 14:6)

PHOTO © Susan Roberts

FIRE ALARM

E-U, E-U, E-U! The fire alarm sounded, accompanied by an annoying, staccato voice warning, "Fire! Fire!" I was boiling water for spaghetti when the oversensitive device sprang into action. I quickly opened all the doors and windows and turned on the ceiling fans. After a few minutes, the noise quit—thankfully. My neighbors must think I am a horrible cook. That false alarm (what harm is there in spaghetti?) required my immediate, full attention.

Some alarms are easier to ignore, yet much more important. God had sent lots of warnings to the Israelites. He had caused floods and famines and sent disease and pestilence. He stirred up wars and sent his people into captivity. God wanted them to turn to him, but they turned their backs instead of their faces (*see* Jeremiah 2:27). "I did all this," God told them through the prophet Amos, "but still you did not return to me" (*see* Amos 4). This sounds uncannily like our country today. Many have turned their backs on God. We sin. We do not acknowledge God. Natural disasters, terrorism and wars have been prevalent. Could it be that God is warning this nation to return to him? Is he poised to pour out his wrath and judgment? This is an alarm that's easy to ignore. We can chalk up our misfortunes to coincidence. Regardless of what you believe about these things, it's time to turn our faces to God. He's deserving of our immediate attention. Let us turn to the Lord.

"O Lord, You are so good and kind, so ready to forgive, so full of mercy for all who ask your aid." (Psalm 86:5, TLB)

PHOTO © Susan Roberts

KEY

It was dark when we arrived at our apartment. How I wished we had a garage door opener to automatically open our door with just the push of a button. Instead I had to enter our block of apartments through an outside hallway and, reaching our front door, fumble with my keys. The area was poorly lit, making it hard to see the keyhole; and the key didn't fit smoothly, either. I had to set down the bags in my arms. After a few unsuccessful attempts, I finally pulled out my cell phone and used the flashlight app to better see the slot. Finally, the key aligned perfectly and turned. The door opened.

Often I have wished for a button that would automatically open heaven's door and give us access to God's bounty. I have not found prayer to work that way, though. We can't push a button to get what we want or need from God. Our mind and spirit need to be perfectly aligned with God, and that takes work. We may not see him very clearly. The light of God's truth, shed into our hearts by the Holy Spirit helps us. We also may need to set aside the baggage of sin and self that we carry, so that we are free to focus on God's purposes. God loves us, his beloved children, and desires to give us good things. But he also desires for us to seek him and know him so he can do what is best for us. Let us align ourselves to God, surrendered fully to him. Let us pray fervently for God's will be done.

"If we ask anything according to his will, he hears us." (1 John 5:14)

PHOTO © Susan Roberts

PUTTING AWAY CHRISTMAS

Sometimes cold weather and snow delay the removal of Christmas lights and outdoor decorations. In our neighborhood, they are usually gone by New Year's Day, but sometimes they remain all the way until February. I am not complaining. I love the festive lights; they remind me of the joy of this season. I am always a bit sad to see them disappear.

Even though we can't get to our outdoor decorations just yet, we are slowly, but surely, removing our indoor decorations—packing up ornaments, dishes and décor. This task is a bit melancholy, but we like getting our house back in order.

As we packed up our nativity scene, placing it back in its box, I thought, even as this visual reminder of Jesus' coming was put away, that I did not have to put away the meaning and spirit of the season. The impact of it could remain in my mind and spirit.

This year, as we return to our usual routine, let's allow the spirit of Christmas to remain. Let's not "put away" Jesus or his light. We must tuck him into our hearts, drawing on his forgiveness, love, power, comfort, and guidance. Let the light of Christmas shine in us and through us the whole year through.

"For God, who said, 'Let light shine out of darkness,' made his light shine in our hearts to give us the light of the knowledge of God's glory displayed in the face of Christ." (2 Corinthians 4:6)

PHOTO © Dr. Marc Yasoni

TIME

Here's a riddle I wrote as a poem:

> What gift are you given that you cannot hold?
> It's priceless, yet free, never earned, I am told.
> You want it, yet waste it, as it slips away,
> You spend it, you save it, not for the next day.
> It runs fast and slow, but will never rest.
> You dread it, yet love it, when it's at its best.
> You mark it, you keep it, but lose it you will.
> Yet, remarkably it keeps replenishing still.
> Someday it is gone, you must bid it adieu,
> So use wisely what has been given to you!"

The answer, of course, is time. The gift of time is a precious commodity. When we think there is a lot of something, it becomes devalued. But we don't know how much time we have. One's earthly life can end in an instant. A person with a terminal illness is generally more thoughtful about using their remaining time to make a difference. Their priorities fall into place. Live each day as if it were your last, making it count.

"Lord, help me to realize how brief my time on earth will be. Help me to know that I am here for but a moment more." (Psalm 39:4, TLB)

PHOTO © Susan Roberts

RESTORING THE SHINE

It just looked dull. I had finished mopping the floor, but there was no sparkle. It was clean, but I wondered what I could do to make it look better. After some trial and error, I found a product that revived the shine. What a difference. The floor looked great.

We Christians clean up our act, confessing our sin, and are forgiven—washed clean in God's eyes. But, to the world's eyes, we may look pretty dull. We can get caught up in legalism, judgment and criticism as we try to clean up the dirt in our world. That is hardly the way to let our light shine.

So, what will restore our shine? Do you remember the story of Moses going up Mt. Sinai to get God's law? When he returned, he was glowing. Why? Because he had been with God. We may not glow quite like Moses did; but spending time with God does increase our shine. Shine is a reflection of God—others seeing God in us.

I want to sparkle like jewels in a crown, and shine like the stars in the sky (*see* Zechariah 9:16-17). So I'm working on my shine.

"Do everything without grumbling or arguing, so that you may become blameless and pure, children of God without fault in a warped and crooked geeration. Then you will shine among them like stars in the sky as you hold firmly to the word of life." (Philippians 2:14-16)

PHOTO © Susan Roberts

GIFTS

It is fun to receive gifts. The anticipation and excitement of ripping off the wrapping is almost as much fun as the gift itself. But what if you do not trust the gift giver? You may be nervous about opening the present, thinking of impending disappointment, or anger at the gift's inappropriateness. Such fear takes away the fun.

I have recently heard people talking about their fears. Some fear their financial situation. Others fear what will happen in the future with retirement or their health. The world situation and terrorism cause some to be uneasy. Parents worry about their kids' safety, choices, and future. We don't know what's in store, but we do know that each of our days is a gift from God, waiting to be unwrapped. We can approach each day tentatively with trepidation and lack of trust, or we can eagerly "rip off the wrappings," day by day, with anticipation and excitement. James tells us that "every good and perfect gift is from above" (James 1:17).

We can trust him to provide good gifts that are always just what we need—always appropriate. We can replace our fear with faith.

"Which of you, if his son asks him for bread, will give him a stone? Or if he asks for a fish, will give him a snake? If you, then, though you are evil, know how to give good gifts to your children, how much more will your Father in heaven give good gifts to those who ask him." (Matthew 7:9-11)

PHOTO © Susan Roberts

MAKING CHILI

As the weather grows chilly, I think of making chili. One time, at my husband's sister's house, she added all the ingredients according to the chili recipe and put the pot on the stove. As it boiled, it began to froth and expand. We put it in two pots, then three, then four. It smelled and tasted terrible. She added more hamburger, more spices and more tomatoes—all the good stuff. It kept expanding and frothing, and the taste didn't improve. Finally, after several hours of cooking and trying to remedy the "mess," we gave up and threw it out, burying it in the garden. Their dog later dredged it up, ate it and got sick! We determined the problem must have been a few beans she threw in the pot. They had not been dried property, and though there were only a few, they tainted the whole pot.

That's the way it is with sin. You can do lots of good stuff, keep adding more, but a little sin—malice, greed, impurity, etc. can taint the effectiveness we have. Corporately, sin can hurt our church. Paul reminds us in 1 Corinthians 5:6 and again in Galatians 5:9 that a little yeast leavens the whole lump. A little sin harms you as an individual and the church as a whole.

Instead, as you follow God's recipe for life, make sure, with his help, you get rid of the bad stuff and use all the right stuff so that you positively, not negatively, affect those around you.

"The kingdom of heaven is like yeast that a woman took and mixed into a large amount of flour until it worked all through the dough." (Matthew 13:33)

PHOTO © Susan Roberts

THAT DOESN'T BELONG

We are decorating for Christmas—hanging lights, tying bows and wrapping garlands. I stand back to look and, to my chagrin, I notice something I had overlooked. There on our front door, sticking out like a sore thumb, is our fall wreath—complete with gourds and pumpkins. It certainly looks out of place!

This season I have noticed many things that are out of place. This is supposed to be a time of joy, peace and love, as we celebrate the Giver of those gifts to us. But, instead, a driver impatiently cuts someone off because he thought they were going too slow on icy roads; a shopper aggressively pushes ahead in line, casting hateful looks at the others around her; moms and dads bark at their kids, out of their own frustration and impatience. It seems everyone is too hurried and hassled to lend a hand to anyone in need. All around us, in people's attitudes and actions, Christ is taken out of Christmas. In effect, even advertisers remove Christ as they tout "holiday" items instead.

We should be looking for ways to spread the good will and peace that the angels announced at Jesus' birth—like the neighbor who quietly shoveled our walk after the snowstorm. We have Jesus to empower and encourage us! May our Christmas truly reflect Jesus! In all you do, put Christ back in Christmas. That's his place.

"May the God who gives endurance and encouragement give you a spirit of unity among yourselves as you follow Christ Jesus." (Romans 15:5)

PHOTO © Susan Roberts

SNOW CREATIONS

A snowstorm hit the same day our two little grandsons came to visit. They love the snow. When the sun came out, we went outside to sled; then we made snow angels and sculptures. For these little boys, snowmen didn't cut it—too sissy and ordinary. So, we made a snow shark! They were quite proud of their creation, and we all admired their handiwork.

The next day, even though it was still cold outside, they ran outside to see their shark but were disappointed. The sun had begun to destroy their work. The snow angels had become too distorted to recognize. The snow shark lost its fin. Then snow began to fall again and covered everything, looking as if nothing had ever been there.

What we do in this life will vanish. What seemed like a great accomplishment at the time, will eventually become insignificant. Even our lives are but a vapor, a flower quickly fading, here today, gone tomorrow. That's why Jesus told us to lay up eternal treasures and spend our time on things of eternal value (see Matthew 6:20). These will not be destroyed. A poem by CT Studd declares, "Only one life, will soon be past. Only what's done for Christ will last." As we approach the New Year, let us consider what we can do that will be of eternal value.

"Each one who builds must be very careful....Everyone's work will be put through the fire so that all can see whether or not it keeps its value, and what was really accomplished." (1 Corinthians 3:10-13, TLB)

PHOTO © Cathy Lyoms

BUILDING SNOWMEN

Around the world, building snowmen is a popular activity. Did you know one of the first recorded snowmen was built by Michelangelo—at age nineteen—for the ruler of Florence, Italy? The Swiss, in Zurich, have a longstanding tradition called *Sechselauten*. On the third Monday in April, a cotton snowman called a *Boogg*, is filled with dynamite and paraded through town to the place where a pile of wood has been stacked for a bonfire. The snowman tops the wood, which is then lit, and the ensuing boom heralds the end of winter and the start of spring. In Brussels during the winter of 1511, an unfortunate snowman event occurred. After a particularly cold, snowy January, people enjoyed building snowmen all over town. Lots of them. A sudden thaw in mid February melted the snowmen too suddenly, causing a flood. The people had not considered the cost of their endeavor.

In Luke chapter 14 Jesus told a parable about a builder who was about to build a tower. He first had to consider the cost, otherwise he might have run out of funds and not have completed his task. It may seem pleasant to enjoy God's love and grace and not consider the cost of being a Christ follower. Although we are freed from the penalty of sin, let us not forget that we have become "slaves to righteousness" (Romans 6:16). As we celebrate the wonder of God's free love and grace, let us not forget to consider the cost.

> "As obedient children, do not conform to the evil desires you had when you lived in ignorance. But just as he who called you is holy, so be holy in all you do."

PHOTO © Susan Roberts

LOTTERY TICKETS

Our son-in-law had often purchased lottery tickets. Once when he stopped for gas on his way home, he went into the store to pay and pick up his customary ticket, when he heard God speak to his heart: "If you purchase this lottery ticket, you will win, but it will have a negative impact on you and your family." He decided not to buy the ticket and has not bought one since. The security of his family, and being obedient to God's voice were more important to him than the lure of wealth.

I thought about this recently when I read about Balaam in Numbers chapter 22. Balak, King of Moab, offered to reward him handsomely if only he would curse the Israelites so they wouldn't defeat Moab. Balaam wavered until God sent a donkey and an angel to warn him to follow God's directive. "Even if Balak gave me all the silver and gold in his palace, I could not do anything great or small to go beyond the command of the Lord my God," Balaam decided. Balak continued to try to persuade Balaam by offering sacrifices in various places, but Balaam stood his ground. Even though his words put him in jeopardy, Balaam refused to curse whom God had blessed.

Following God's leading is far more important than material gain. Be careful. Don't be lured by earthly pleasures or riches, away from what God would have you do or say. God may not send an angel and a donkey to put you on the right course, but he will speak.

"Did I not tell you that I must do whatever the Lord says?' Balaam replied."
(Numbers 23:26)

PHOTO © Chris Roberts

STORIES

Who doesn't love stories?

My husband is a great storyteller and has quite a repertoire of experiences to share. When each of us was little, both he and I enjoyed hearing about our parents when they were kids. How different life was back then, without all the technology!

Stories using humorous anecdotes or jokes make us smile. Sad or inspirational tales tug at our heart strings. Stories teach us about life, other cultures, and history. They help us speculate about the "what ifs."

The best story ever told comes from the Bible. We can learn about God, his interaction with people and his amazing love shown in sending his Son. As God interacts with us, we each develop personal stories of his faithfulness, love, and transforming power. These are the best stories to tell.

Spread the news. Make it personal. People may be put off by proselytizing and theology. But they love stories. What is God doing in your life?

What is your story to tell?

> "Since my youth, O God, You have taught me, and to this day I declare your marvelous deeds. Even when I am old and gray, do not forsake me, O God, till I declare your power to the next generation, and your might to all who are to come." (Psalm 71:17-18)

PHOTO © Perry Roberts

CHOCOLATE MESS

I have a sweet tooth. Chocolate is my nemesis. When my husband contracted MS, we went on a strict diet that cut out all carbohydrates and sugar. At first the cravings were nearly impossible to manage. I even dreamt about chocolate. But after a while, our bodies adjusted and we actually got to the point where we felt sick if we ate sweets. We craved fresh fruits and veggies instead, and we actually felt better.

Each of us has cravings—for something—that are hard to keep in check. Yet, when we deny these longings, they eventually diminish. This is a good thing in regard to unhealthy desires. However, we are meant to yearn for the things we need. We have been called to hunger and thirst after righteousness. How do we do that? By conscientiously adding spiritual food to our daily diet by "supping" with God. This may be difficult at first; we don't desire it. New habits are hard to develop. We will eventually get to the point where, like David, we say, "As a deer pants for the streams of water, so my soul pants for you, my God" (Psalm 42:1). When we make him the pattern for our lives, we crave God's presence. But if we crave worldly things, those will consume us and lead us to destruction. If we Christians want to have an impact on our world, we must begin with ourselves—developing our hunger and thirst for righteousness and allowing God to change our cravings from worldly to godly. Then who knows what God will do in and through us?

> "Blessed are those who hunger and thirst for righteous, for they will be filled."
> (Matthew 5:6)

PHOTO © Perry Roberts

THOMAS THE TRAIN

The family room floor was a mess. We had fit train track pieces together and expanded the route to cover the entire floor. There was hardly a patch of bare carpet. Our grandson is crazy about trains. When we visited, we spent hours playing on the floor with him. At bedtime, he put on his "Thomas the Train" PJs and we settled down to watch his favorite "Thomas the Train" cartoon. In this particular episode, one of the trains had to deliver some coal quickly. The bridge was out so he was forced to take an alternate route through the "Whistling Wood." The train insisted on doing it alone so the other trains wouldn't think he was a scaredy cat. Three times he tried to do it alone, but each time, he became frightened and hurried backwards out of the forest. He finally accepted help from the others. They had been through the forest before and knew the way and what to expect.

Rev. Wilbert Auwdry created Thomas the Train and the stories for his son Christopher. The simple life lessons are not only helpful for kids but amazingly apropos to adult life also. Who among us has not had to tackle a daunting task that makes us afraid? We cannot see through "the trees," and have to approach the challenge blindly. But we don't have to do it alone! God is with us always and will strengthen and help us. We can also lay aside our pride and accept the assistance of others who "have been there."

"And let us consider how we may spur one another on toward love and good deeds, not giving up meeting together, as some are in the habit of doing, but encouraging one another—and all the more as you see the Day approaching."
(Hebrews 10:24-25)

PHOTO © Susan Roberts

COFFEE

My husband and I love our coffee in the morning! The day just doesn't seem right without the warm wake-up of our favorite brew. Even the aroma gets us moving! We received one of those Keurig® coffee makers and have enjoyed experimenting with lots of different flavors from the multiple options available. A little cup of potential goes in along with a tank of water, and voilà!—out comes a perfectly brewed cup! Sometimes we want more than the minimal, so we still occasionally brew a whole pot.

I desire to look forward to my prayer time with the same anticipation that I have for our morning cup of coffee. I believe that prayer is of the utmost importance. Yes, I should have even more of a yearning for this important aspect of my spiritual life!

Prayer should be a habit that we are not inclined to do without—our warmth and wake-up every day. We are the cup of potential, waiting for God's Spirit to flow in and through us. When we pray, the Holy Spirit pours his living water into our lives and out comes the wonderful flavors of his fruit, and the sweet aroma of Jesus. Let's not be satisfied with the minimal, but immerse ourselves wholly in God. Great Christians such as Billy Graham have been great pray-ers. If we want to stand firm and make a difference, let's start each morning on our knees.

"In the morning, O Lord, you hear my voice; in the morning I lay my requests before you and wait in expectation." (Psalm 5:3)

PHOTO © Kent Nelson

PEARL HARBOR

A few years ago, we visited Pearl Harbor and the USS Arizona Memorial. The remnants of all the wrecked ships are still visible beneath the water's surface. A huge number of fallen servicemen's names are inscribed on a wall inside the memorial. It was sobering to see family members' tears, even after all these years, as they wept for their fallen heroes. But we also felt a sense of pride. These brave men and women did not die in vain. Their deaths were the spark that kindled the resolve to take charge and be victorious. As we toured the harbor, we learned about the courage of those who remained. In spite of their debilitating losses, they worked tirelessly to repair the damage and prepare for the next battle. They had ships and planes up and running in record time.

We too can feel defeated by the curve balls life throws at us, and it is hard to get up and keep going. But we have God's power that is perfected in weakness. We have strength that enables us to do all things. "Greater is he who is in us, than he who is in the world" (1 John 4:4). You can be victorious. Hang in there. Persevere. God is with you.

"But we have this treasure in jars of clay to show that this all-surpassing power is from God and not from us. We are hard pressed on every side, but not crushed; perplexed, but not in despair; persecuted, but not abandoned; struck down, but not destroyed." (2 Corinthians 4:7-9)

PHOTO © Dr. Ed Holroyd

ADVENT

Beginning at the end of November, many families prepare for Christmas by celebrating Advent. The word Advent means coming. It literally comes from the Latin "ad" meaning "to that place" and "veni" meaning "to come." Jesus is coming to that place called earth.

It is said that Martin Luther was in the hills surrounding his village one evening near Christmas. As he contemplated the advent, he noticed the fir trees which were silhouetted against the starry sky, looking like Christmas trees. He thought that the Christmas tree was a good illustration of Jesus' coming. For Christmas, the tree gives up its lofty home to come down into our homes, giving up its life. It is evergreen, symbolizing everlasting life. A single top branch points the one way to God and each bough, with its perpendicular branches, forms the shape of a cross.

During this Christmas season, look around you. You may notice many things that remind you of Jesus' coming too. Christmas trees are not the only telltale symbol. Listen to the rich theology in carols. Look for ornaments with biblical parallels like stars, angels and even apples and trumpets. What will you discover? Jesus coming to earth is what Christmas is all about.

"Christ Jesus: Who being in very nature God, did not consider equality with God something to be grasped, but made himself nothing, taking the very nature of a servant ... humbled himself and became obedient to death—even death on a cross!" (Philippians 2:5-8)

PHOTO © Susan Roberts

CHRISTMAS VILLAGE

Every year we set up a Christmas village. Our kids have added pieces to it over the years, until it has become quite elaborate. We finally said, "Enough, already." This year however, since our grandson loves trains, we bought an electric train for the village. The box did not say that it had sound. It obnoxiously repeats over and over, "All aboard for the Santa Express! Merry Christmas!" An off-tune rendition of "Jingle Bells" plays in the background. We want to figure out a way to disable the sound, but so far have been unsuccessful.

There are a lot of obnoxious things about this season that we wish would go away. A friend expressed how much she hates Christmas because of rude family members getting together and fighting. Another said it is hard because she is alone—no family around, and everyone else is preoccupied with theirs. One of my neighbors complained about the traffic, long lines and grumpy people. She said that she hates to go out and now only shops online. Stress and financial strains, loneliness and overcrowded schedules can sap the joy from a season designed for joy and peace. I heard a radio DJ say, "You might not be able to make things go away, or turn it off; but you can change the channel."

Fix your eyes on Jesus. That's what the season is all about. It is not about what you are doing or even what is done to you, but about what was done for you. Jesus came and did it all. That completes our joy and peace.

"But he has appeared once for all at the end of the ages to do away with sin by the sacrifice of himself." (Hebrews 9:26)

PHOTO © CanStockPhoto Inc / slickspics

I HAVE A DREAM

"I have a dream." You may recognize this iconic phrase from a speech of Martin Luther King, Jr. whose birthday we celebrate each January. He left the legacy of a call to brotherhood and equality, which set a standard of behavior and legislation that has shaped the direction of our country. We have a long way to go, but we have also seen remarkable progress.

What is the legacy you are building? What is your dream? We probably won't get a national holiday to commemorate our birthdays, but we can lay up treasure in heaven and look forward to God's affirmation: "Well done, you good and faithful servant" (Matthew 25:21).

Our church choir sang a song by Ruth Elain Schram: "Make My Life an Alleluia, A song of praise to you each day." What better legacy to leave than one that points not to ourselves and what we have accomplished, but to God, giving him the glory. May our lives reflect who God is and the wonderful things that he is doing. May we be an ever-airing anthem of praise that continues even after we have left this place for our new home. When people think of us, may they not think of who we are or were, but who God is.

"But I will sing of your strength, in the morning I will sing of your love; for you are my fortress, my refuge in times of trouble." (Psalm 59:16-17)

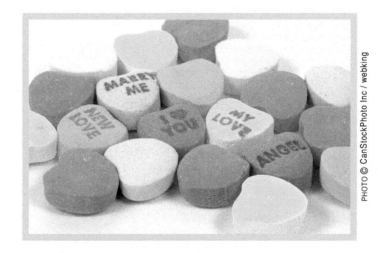

PHOTO © CanStockPhoto Inc / webking

VALENTINE'S DAY

Let's go out for dinner and dancing. Or maybe we should stay home and eat by candlelight. Couples try to think of romantic ways to celebrate Valentine's Day, but for some, it is a hard time of feeling unloved or having lost in love. Tina Turner, back in the early nineties, experienced the pain and disappointment of love lost as she escaped from an abusive marriage. She became self-centered, hardened, and cynical. She wrote a song, "What's Love Got To Do With It?" that asked the questions: "What's love but a second-hand emotion? Who needs a heart when a heart can be broken?" In spite of her success, she was a very unhappy person in her life and in her marriage. This is a classic example of how fame and fortune do not bring happiness.

But, love has everything to do with it! It is not just love of a spouse, friends and family. They can disappoint, let us down, or be taken from us. We can hang onto God's love which is sure (*see* Romans 8:38-39). God's love does not disappoint, nor is it based on circumstances or our actions. We are loved unconditionally. Resting in the confidence of God's all-encompassing love for us does bring happiness, peace, and satisfaction. Being filled with God's love in our spirits enables us to pass that love along. It overflows. God sends you a message from heaven: I love you. Be mine.

"I have loved you with an everlasting love!" (Jeremiah 31:3)

PHOTO © Susan Roberts

ST. PATRICK'S DAY

Happy St. Patrick's Day! Did you know there are nine times more people of Irish heritage in the USA than in all of Ireland? On March 17 we honor St. Patrick, whose real name was Maewyn Succat. He was born in Britain but was kidnapped and taken to Ireland as a slave. There he worked primarily as a sheepherder. He later escaped and returned to Britain, where he became a priest and changed his name to Patrick. In a vision God told him to return to Ireland to bring Christianity to a people who had never heard the message of salvation. He obeyed. Talk about forgiveness! As he taught the pagans about God and Jesus, he used a shamrock to explain the trinity. That image helped them begin to grasp the concept of our three-in-one God.

St. Patrick's Day in the USA is associated with revelry, drinking, fun and eating corned beef. But it is really a serious religious holiday, occurring in the middle of lent on the anniversary of Patrick's death. Use this time to reflect on spreading the gospel to those who have not heard, and eradicating sin through confession and repentance. Take a moment to confess your sin and contemplate Jesus' forgiveness. In the spirit of St. Patrick, reflect on how you can take the incredible message of salvation to someone who has not heard this Good News.

"Therefore go and make disciples of all nations, baptizing them in the name of the Father and of the Son and of the Holy Spirit, and teaching them to obey everything I have commanded you." (Matthew 28:19)

SPRING

PHOTO © Susan Roberts

THE JOURNEY

We are in the process of planning a trip. It's many months away, and we could easily procrastinate. But we have learned by experience to address the details of our travel plans early. Otherwise, things will be booked or cost more.

We've been accused of over planning and not allowing for the "whatevers." We have friends who like spontaneity. They have taken trips without even knowing the destination. They just flip a coin at each intersection: heads is right, tails is left. Sometimes their adventures are quite rewarding. Other times they are disappointing, and they have even gone in circles. Though they hate to admit it, even their whimsical, free-spirited trips require planning—taking time off, filling the gas tank, and packing for all the contingencies. Even they cannot just wake up one day and take off unprepared.

Christians are planning for a spiritual trip. We know that someday we will be traveling to heaven—either when we pass on, or when Jesus comes for us. It might seem so far off that we have trouble grasping the reality, and keeping focused. We don't know the day or hour, so we don't know how much time we have to plan. Though we have our "tickets," we get caught up in our earthly affairs and forget the most important preparedness for eternity. Jesus warns us in parable of "the virgins and the lamps," to watch and not be caught off guard. Whether you like to live spontaneously or in purposeful attention to details, what you do now will prepare you for your journey to eternity.

"Therefore keep watch because you do not know the day or the hour."
(Matthew 25:13)

PHOTO © Susan Roberts

FEED THE GOOD ONE

Feeding ostriches is dangerous. They towered above our SUV at nine feet, and were particularly aggressive. As we drove through the wildlife park, we first saw the ostriches, who were very anxious for a bite of cracker. Our open windows were an invitation for one of the ostriches to snake its whole neck and head into our car and help itself to the contents of our dashboard. When our daughter tried to shoo him away, the creature bit her finger. We became much more cautious, only leaving the window open a crack, unnerved by that rude fellow.

When I was growing up, my Mom had two little dog-shaped magnets. One was "good." One was "bad." She used them as a lesson to teach me and my sister to invest in righteousness rather than evil. She told us that the one we "fed" would be the most powerful. If we fed the good one, we would enjoy the benefits of love, joy, peace, and goodness. If we focused on the bad one, we would succumb to bitterness, anger, impatience, and hatred. "Watch out which one you feed!" she would warn.

If we choose to encourage the less desirable, we will get bitten. Let us instead choose to cultivate the good things in our lives.

> "But if serving the Lord seems undesirable to you, then choose for yourselves this day whom you will serve....But as for me and my household, we will serve the Lord." (Joshua 24:15)

PHOTO © Susan Roberts

DEEP, DARK, BLACK CANYON

Thousands of years ago, the Gunnison River in western Colorado set its course across soft volcanic rock, carving its way eventually into hard metamorphic rock. The swift running water created the steep walls of the Black Canyon—the fifth steepest gorge in the US—even beating out the Grand Canyon for sheer drops. This narrow gorge gets only about thirty-three minutes of sunlight a day, keeping it in darkness—thus its name.

Rushing waters have remarkable impact on surrounding landscapes, carving rock into canyons such as this, changing the course of rivers, and at flood stage, uprooting trees and moving rocks and soil. Even a little water can gradually split cracks in rocks, breaking them into pieces.

One of the images the Bible gives us of Jesus is that of Living Water (see John 4:10-13). He indeed has the power to break down hard hearts, change the course of lives, sweep away the debris and dirt of sin, and remove obstacles to faith. Sometimes he acts like a flood, working dramatically and quickly. Sometimes it is the constant erosion over time that eventually breaks down our hardened hearts. Let us allow his work in our lives to mold us and shape us into what he wants us to be. Let us also pray that his Living water will be at work in those around us to seep in and bring change.

> "Yet, O Lord, you are our Father. We are the clay, you are the potter; we are all the work of your hand." (Isaiah 64:8)

PHOTO © Jeff Osterlund

SHADOWS

Sunrise is a great time to visit the Colorado National Monument near Grand Junction. We found a wonderful overlook facing the valley to the east, filled with rock walls and pinnacles. As the sun rose, the sky filled with color and the rocks reflected the light, making spectacular shadows. We *ooohed* and *aahed* at the sunrise but then turned around and laughed at our skinny, distorted images stretching before us. With our backs to the sun, we had fun taking silly pictures of our shadows.

At times we face valleys of shadows, but these are not funny. Big, threatening unknowns of disease, uncertainty, failure and death stretch before us. When Rick Warren was interviewed by Piers Morgan[4] about the untimely death of his son, he talked about the difficulty of walking through the valley of the shadow of death. He observed that when he looked at the shadow, not only was it big and distorted, but his back was to the light. Psalm 23:4 tells us that we can walk through the valley of the shadows and fear no evil because God is with us. Don't focus on the shadow. Turn around and look at the Son instead. Psalm 23 goes on to say that he comforts us and takes care of our needs. If you are facing shadows today, turn around. Jesus is there for you.

"God is our refuge and strength, an ever-present help in trouble. Therefore, we will not fear..." (Psalm 46:1-2)

4. Kate Shellnutt, "Rick Warren Tells Story of Son's Suicide On CNN," *Christianity Today.* http://www.christianitytoday.com/gleanings/2013/september/rick-warren-tells-story-son-matthew-suicide-cnn.html. Accessed 10-26-2016.

PHOTO © Susan Roberts

WALKING IN THE TRACKS

The four-wheel drive vehicles lined up in the parking lot behind the tour guide's truck. On this beautiful spring day, we headed down the dusty, bumpy dirt road into Picketwire Canyon, near La Junta, Colorado. Along the Purgatory River, running through the canyon, are dried mud flats. On them are recorded the steps of ancient travelers. This is the longest set of continual dinosaur tracks in North America. It is amazing to see these distinct tracks preserved in mud, and walk where dinosaurs walked.

Ray Vander Laan, moderator of the "That the World May Know" DVD series filmed in Israel, emphasizes how awesome it is to visit the Holy Land and walk where Jesus walked. He says that only a few people have the privilege of walking "where" Jesus walked, but all of us can walk "how" he walked. Jesus told a parable of the Good Samaritan who showed love to another at considerable personal cost. This is exactly what Jesus did. We are leaving our own set of footprints in the lives of others. Let us make sure that we do walk as Jesus walked.

"If anyone obeys his word, God's love is truly made complete in him. This is how we know we are in him: Whoever claims to live in him must walk as Jesus did." (1 John 2:5-6)

PHOTO © Susan Roberts

THAT DARN POT HOLE

By mistake, I drove over a rather large rut in the road. I didn't see it coming. I was relieved that this lurking pothole didn't cause damage to my car. But it sure shook me up. I think this past winter has been particularly hard on roads. There is road construction everywhere, repairing damage done by the freezes. I saw on the news that there is even a hotline phone number to call to report potholes. It seems to take an awfully long time to get the job done, though.

Things have crept into my spiritual life causing bumps in my road. Hurts leave holes in my spirit. Satan tries to distract me so I do not see the pitfalls of my choices. Difficulties shake me up and rattle my faith.

It is so important to remember that we have a God who restores us. He repairs the hurts and heals the brokenness. He defeats the efforts of Satan. He guides us in the ways we should go. He gives us strength in tough times. Though he may not be working in our lives as quickly as we would like, he is faithful to repair life's damage and continually renew our lives. Call on him to report the damage. Wait on him. He will get the job done. Don't be shaken, for he is faithful.

"I have set the Lord always before me. Because he is at my right hand, I will not be shaken." (Psalm 16:8)

PHOTO © Chris Roberts

WALKING THE DOG

Our apartment complex allows dogs, so every evening we see a parade of pet owners showing off every breed and mixed breed imaginable: big dogs, little dogs, fat dogs, skinny dogs, black dogs, brown dogs, white dogs and spotted dogs. Even a corgi-lab mix. Some dogs strain at the leash, pulling their owner in the true spirit of the Iditarod. Others vacillate from side to side, sniffing (and marking) everything they see. A friend calls this "reading the doggy newspaper." Then there are the well trained dogs walking obediently next to their owner, exemplifying the proper concept of "heel."

We are like these dogs. Yes, we as Christians are saved by grace and free from the law of sin and death, but as Romans says, we become "slaves to righteousness." We are "leashed" by the precepts of God's Word lest we run off and get ourselves into trouble. Some of us rebelliously and defiantly pull at that leash, trying desperately to go our own way. Others have lots of trouble with focus, wandering all over the place, doing this and that, and expending a lot more time and energy than is necessary. Finally, there are those who have learned to submit to our master and walk obediently beside him.

God knows what is best for us, and when we walk with him, we are empowered to be holy and effective, fully carrying out his plan for us. It is only through his leading that we can find the right path.

> "Don't you know that when you offer yourselves to someone to obey him as slaves, you are slaves of the one whom you obey...But thanks be to God that, though you used to be slaves to sin, you have come to obey from your heart..."
> (Romans 6:16-17, NIVUK)

PHOTO © Susan Roberts

NO HANDS

The silver-black sedan stopped at the intersection. When the light turned green, the car lurched forward accelerating quickly from 0 mph to 60 mph. We were riding in a Tesla. Our son-in-law, the driver, had attended a class to learn about the car's features. He tentatively released his hands from the steering wheel to see what it could do. It followed the lines in the road, taking curves, changing lanes, adjusting speed according to speed limit signs, and stopping and starting—all by itself! It even parks itself, opening and closing the garage door with its sensors. It took our son-in-law a long time to trust the car. Taking his hands off the wheel was scary, even though he had heard the reports, seen the videos, read the manual and experienced it in action. It just didn't seem advisable to relinquish control.

Giving up control is tough. We don't want to give God control of our lives either. We like doing it ourselves. We've read his manual, the Bible, we've heard the reports of how he works, and we've even seen God in action ourselves. But the bottom line is we like to be in charge. I once saw a marquee that read, "If God is your copilot, then who is in the driver's seat?" Yes, I like to be in the driver's seat, with hands on the wheel, God by my side. But, God wants us to let him work. He wants our full trust. He wants to show us the way, guiding and helping us through all the obstacles. Let go and let God.

> "Some trust in chariots and some in horses, but we trust in the name of the Lord our God." (Psalm 20:7)

PHOTO © Susan Roberts

IS THE JAR FULL?

My professor friend instructed a group of business students on time management. He took a jar and placed some large rocks inside, filling the jar. "Is the jar full?" he asked. The more astute students recognized that it was not. Then he poured in some small gravel. "Is it full?" No, not yet. Next he poured in sand. Certainly it now appeared full, and most students agreed that he was finished. However, he took a glass of water and poured that in as well. "So, what is the point?" he queried. One student offered, "You can always make room in your schedule for something more." "No," the professor answered. "You must figure out what the big rocks are in your life and attend to them first. Otherwise, the little stuff will get in the way and you will not be able to address the really important things."

So, what are your big rocks? If we are not careful, the tyranny of the urgent will take control and we will not have time for the things that really matter. We were advised to make a list of our priorities: spending time with God in prayer and study, spending time with friends and family, taking time to rest and refresh. Then, schedule these things and do not waiver. If our lives are too busy with non priorities, it may be time to adjust our activities. Let us all entreat God to help us rightly identify how we should use our time.

"He will be the sure foundation for your times, a rich store of salvation and wisdom and knowledge; the fear of the Lord is the key to this treasure." (Isaiah 33:6)

PHOTO © Pat Burdick

IN A FOG

All we could see before us were ghostly shapes, barely visible in the fog. It was hard going across the lake, for the way was almost obscured by the wafts of mist. Fog horns groaned a warning of their approaching ships and we peered ahead to avoid a collision. With no GPS and few reference points, finding our destination was a challenge. We felt relief when the fog finally lifted and we could see.

Our future, even our day's path, is often obscured like this. Sometimes we have glimpses of the way we should go, but at times we might not see our way at all, and are unsure about choices or actions. If we stay in tune with the Holy Spirit's prompting, he will guide our way, a step at a time. We might not see, but we can hear his voice. Jesus says, "My sheep listen to my voice; I know them and they follow me" (John 10:27). Each day, as you come to God in scripture and prayer, ask for the Holy Spirit to guide your steps that day, moment by moment. Then, when you "hear" his gentle prompting throughout the day—a nudge, an idea, a thought, a person that pops into your head, do what he says. If you are unsure, ask him again. If it seems particularly "out there," get advice from a spouse or friend, and ask them to pray with you. These little steps help us learn to be attuned to God's bigger plans for us. Don't ignore the leading of the Holy Spirit! This is what makes the Christian life especially rewarding!

"Why do you call me, 'Lord, Lord,' and do not do what I say?...Come to me and hear my words and put them into practice" (Luke 6:45-47).

PHOTO © Dr. Ed Holroyd

WHAT HAPPENED TO MY BULBS?

Those darn varmints! They are wreaking havoc in my garden! A few years ago I planted over 100 crocus bulbs in one of my flower beds. After a couple of years, not one came up. I discovered I had a vole problem. The little critters had not eaten the whole bulb, but had just nibbled on each one enough to destroy its root so it would not sprout. These little guys are cute, but certainly not welcome in my garden! I looked into vole eradication solutions and found numerous repellents and poisons. Even the exterminators said that the problem was next to impossible to remedy. I also found I could protect my bulbs by encasing them in a fine wire mesh before planting, or even use an empty yogurt container with holes punched in it as a barrier. These blockades should prevent the voles from attacking my bulbs.

Like the bulbs, we often have the stuff of life nibbling at us and destroying our ability to grow and flower. Things like bitterness, anger, fear, anxiety and discontentment can make us unproductive. Ephesians 4:31 says to get rid of such things. Jesus tells us in John 15:5 that if we abide in him, we will bear much fruit. If we allow him to encase us in his love and protection, we can grow and produce. Apart from Jesus, we can do nothing. In Jesus, we can bloom where we are planted displaying beautiful flowers of love and peace to those around us.

"Get rid of all bitterness, rage and anger, brawling and slander, along with every form of malice. Be kind and compassionate to one another, forgiving each other, just as in Christ God forgave you." (Ephesians 4:31)

PHOTO © Dr. Ed Holroyd

SPINNING WEBS

I noticed a huge spider web on my deck. Before I smashed it with a broom, I took a moment to admire the artistry. It truly was beautiful. How awesome of God to program this not so tiny spider to do such wonderful, intricate work! Ants and mosquitoes don't spin webs. Neither do raccoons or rabbits. This talent is unique to spiders.

Before the beginning of time, God also planned tasks for us to do. We were uniquely created to do something special! "Now God gives us many kinds of special abilities, but it is the same Holy Spirit who is the source of them all. There are different kinds of service to God, but it is the same Lord we are serving. There are many ways in which God works in our lives, but it is the same God who does the work in and through all of us who are his. The Holy Spirit displays God's power through each of us as a means of helping his entire church" (1 Corinthians 12: 4-6, TLB). No job, no person is less important or less honorable. All of us, with our particular functions, are crucial parts of the whole.

As you head out today, think about how you are putting your unique spin on the things you are doing, and thank God for his wonderful handiwork in making you just as you are!

"For we are God's workmanship, created in Christ Jesus to do good works, which God prepared in advance for us to do." (Ephesians 2:10)

PHOTO © Mike Kepto

THE PREDATOR

I watched a bald eagle flying stealthily across the bay. Suddenly it swooped, scooping up a fish from the dark water below. I have read that eagles have superb eyesight and can see a fish one hundred feet below, even while flapping their wings. They can see a rabbit a mile away while soaring at a thousand feet, and spot a target in a three square mile area. They are very good at catching their prey.

We sometimes forget that there is a predator out there, stalking about to see which of us he can devour (*see* I Peter 5:8). He also is very good at what he does. Satan is indeed alive and well, and very intent on stealing our joy, shaking our faith, filling us with fear and worry, and harming us in any way possible. So, be alert. God has not left us alone to fight by ourselves. He has sent us his Spirit to equip us with power (*see* Acts 1:4-5; 2:39) and has given us his full armor to do battle and stand against the devil's schemes (*see* Ephesians 6:10-12), Put it on. When things *are not* going well, temptation comes. Be vigilant. When things *are* going well, we become overconfident, inattentive, and vulnerable to subtle attacks. Then be especially vigilant.

"Be watchful and control yourselves. Your enemy the devil is like a roaring lion. He prowls about looking for someone to swallow up. Stand up to him. Remain strong in what you believe. You know that you are not alone in your suffering...God always gives you all the grace you need." (1 Peter 5:8-10)

PHOTO © Dr. Mark Yasoni

A STORM IS COMING

The sky turned dark as storm clouds began to build in the south, roiling into impending blackness. Thunder rumbled and lightening flashed. A few drops of rain spattered on the sidewalk.

Our son and his family were staying with us when our cell phones beeped announcing a severe storm warning. We stepped outside. Our son is a pilot and well versed in cloud formations and weather patterns, so he explained to us the technical aspects of the impending storm. He even videotaped the large, rotating cloud formation that can sometimes indicate a tornado. Our four-year-old grandson had seen tornadoes where they live in Little Rock, Arkansas. He was worried that our house would be leveled. We, however, were fascinated with this demonstration of incredible power.

I recalled the way Job and David attributed thunder, lightning and the power of a storm to the awesomeness of God (*see* Job 37; Psalm 135:5-7). We took the opportunity to assure our grandson that our great, powerful God would take care of us. He uses storms to show his might. During the storms of life we can analyze and plan, be anxious and fearful: or we can appreciate and trust in the almighty, omnipotent God who holds thunderbolts in his hand. Our God is not weak. And he loves us. We can trust him.

> "He voice thunders in marvelous ways. He does great things beyond our understanding. He says to the snow, 'Fall on the earth,' and to the rain shower, 'Be a mighty downpour.' So that all men he has made may know his work....He loads the clouds with moisture; he scatters his lightning through them." (Job 37:5-11)

PHOTO © Dr. Ed Holroyd

ZEALOUS PECKING

That woodpecker was at it again, banging on our metal gutters like a jackhammer. He also attacked the siding of our house, poking holes right through to the insulation. Our neighbor dealt with a lot of damage to his stucco walls. I read that flickers use this drumming technique to attract a mate or defend their territory. The metal surfaces make a louder, more impressive noise, but sometimes the flickers get carried away and seem to attack anything in sight. To homeowners, their zeal becomes quite obnoxious and destructive. They continue, purpose driven, without guidance or understanding, working hard and making a mess.

I read about Saul in the book of 1 Samuel. Zealous to attack the Philistines and Gibeonites, he impatiently moved on without God's support. His endeavors were disastrous, eventually ending in his death and the death of his sons.

Our zealousness must align with truth (*see* Romans 10:2). When we charge on, without considering God, our results can be disastrous. Don't be a woodpecker enthusiastically pecking, to no good. Seek God and be zealous for his purposes. Then your zealousness will pay off.

> "Many are the plans in a man's heart, but it is the Lord's purpose that prevails." (Proverbs 19:21)

PHOTO © Karen Burdick

PACKED WITH POWER

The nonstop flight lasts twenty-two hours and covers five-hundred miles across the Gulf of Mexico. The total trip is more than 1000 miles, with a few stops along the way. Tiny ruby-throated hummingbirds migrate this path alone, north from Central America to Colorado, where they arrive at my feeders in late April. They breed in the same locations before migrating south in September. Their little hearts beat 1200 times a minute, and their tiny wings beat over eighty times a second. They can travel at 60 mph. They gorge themselves on bugs, spiders, and nectar to prepare for the arduous journey. God has programmed these tiny creatures with strength and instinct.

Our daughter's family was thrilled when a hummingbird built a nest under their patio roof. The kids called the busy mom Zoom-zoom, watching as she built her chicken-egg sized nest. They observed tiny babies emerge from pea-sized eggs and later learn to fly.

God packs power into small and unassuming things. He has made us fearfully and wonderfully, yet many times we feel frail, unimportant, and impotent. That is precisely when God can use us and give us his strength (*see* 2 Corinthians 12:9). When we feel competent on our own, we easily lose sight of God and go our own way. Then God can't use us or bless us.

Do you need strength today to tackle the tasks before you? Don't rely on yourself. Trust God to provide for your every need.

"For the eyes of the Lord range throughout the earth to strengthen those whose hearts are fully committed to him." (2 Chronicles 16:9)

PHOTO © Susan Roberts

IMITATING THE REAL THING

My family took me to an Italian restaurant for my birthday. I loved the delicious entrée I ordered—so much so that later I checked online, and I found that the restaurant had posted that particular recipe. So I bought the ingredients and carefully followed the instructions, serving it to dinner guests. They raved about this close replica of what I had enjoyed at the restaurant.

I had noticed that some readers responded to the online recipe with suggestions for ways to lower the calorie count, use alternative ingredients, or cut corners for easier preparation. Although the ideas were well-meaning, if I had followed them, this dish wouldn't have turned out like the original.

Paul told the early Christians to be imitators of Christ in life and love (*see* Ephesians 5:1). Some preachers had different ideas, trying to make Christianity more palatable. Paul warned the churches not to follow these alternative ways.

Stick to your guns. Imitate the original. Do not be swayed by false teachers and doctrine. Lots of people today want to tweak Christianity, improve on the premises, make it more relevant, appealing to diversity (*see* 2 Timothy 4:3-4). Let us not be misled. The real recipe for truth is in adherence to God's Word. Don't be fooled by what *sounds* right. God calls the wisdom and logic of this world foolishness (*see* 1 Corinthians 1:20). God's ways are right and perfect. Follow them and things will turn out right.

"Do your best to present yourself to God as one approved, a workman who does not need to be ashamed, and who correctly handles the word of truth."
(2 Timothy 2:15)

PHOTO © Carol Cassell

LEMON BARS

"I hate that dog!" our granddaughter screamed as she walked into the house. Figment, her dog, had been up to no good. Grandma had baked a double batch of lemon bars for her for her birthday. Half went to soccer practice with her, and the final half, with extra lemon topping, remained sitting on the counter. When she got home after practice, every single lemon bar had been eaten, and a very sick dog was none the wiser.

Temptations lure us too. Sometimes we are caught off guard, and sometimes we fully realize the consequences, yet we succumb. Then, we feel awful. How great it is that we are forgiven. Always. Over and over. Nothing can separate us from God's love. When we admit our need of God's help, asking his forgiveness, he is willing to rescue us and provide freedom from the sin addiction that weighs us down and holds us back. Check out Romans 7:14-25 and Hebrews 4:14-16. We can boldly go to God who understands our weaknesses, and find his grace, love and mercy and forgiveness anytime. It has no limits, so great is his love for us.

Our granddaughter forgave Figment. She actually loves him dearly. It helped, of course, that Grandma baked more lemon bars for her.

"For I am convinced that neither death nor life, neither angels nor demons, neither the present nor the future, nor any powers, neither height nor depth, nor anything else in all creation, will be able to separate us from the love of God that is in Christ Jesus our Lord." (Romans 8:38-39)

PHOTO © Susan Roberts

A CLEAR VIEW

We heard strange sounds outside our window—scraping and clanging, whooshing and scratching. We had received a notice that our windows would soon be cleaned, and a peek out the window confirmed that today was the day. The washers worked hard to reach the tough spots. They brought out long poles, buckets and rags. Soon, our windows were sparkling. Prior to them coming, I had noticed the big stuff—the bird splats, the squashed moths, spider webs and mud splatter from the storms, but had not really noticed the subtle film that had built up over time. The clean sparkling windows were a welcome surprise—I can see clearly now, the dirt is gone!

We read a devotion about how we have a window to God. It shows us his grace, love, wisdom and precepts. It can get clouded by our sin, neglect and indifference. Then we can't see well enough to know God and know what he is doing. We might clean up the big stuff that obscures our vision. When we see it, we run to our knees to ask for forgiveness. But over time, the little stuff can gradually cloud our vision. Our secret, unnoticed sins—the little white lie, the contained road rage, the gossip, the impatience or resentment, the pride or selfishness—all can subtly get in the way of our view and mute God's voice. Like David, we need a window cleaning. We need to submit ourselves to God and ask his forgiveness. God's spirit will wash away our sins so we can see clearly.

"Create in me a new, clean heart, O God, filled with clean thoughts and right desires." (Psalm 51:10, TLB)

PHOTO © Susan Roberts

BUILDING

What a conglomeration of boards and plywood. I'm glad experts are building our house, because I wouldn't have the foggiest idea where to begin. It is fun to see it come together, to walk through the framing and envision the rooms and see the views out the windows.

In my devotions, I read about King Solomon building the temple. What a project. He employed 70,000 carriers, 80,000 stonecutters, and 3600 foremen. That was just for the wood and stone. I was glad to see *three* workers at our house. What impressed me about the scriptural account, though, was what Solomon said. What he was building had to be great, because God is greater than all other gods, he said. In awe, Solomon added, "But who is able to build a temple for him, since the heavens, even the highest heavens, cannot contain him?" (2 Chronicles 2:5-6). He thought the temple could hardly be a dwelling place for God. Instead it would be a place to worship and bring him sacrifices—the culmination of their very best efforts, and the very best materials, all done to honor him. And God did choose to dwell in the temple. He chooses to dwell with us, too. He desires relationship with his people. "Don't you know that you yourselves are God's temple and that God's Spirit dwells in your midst?" (1 Corinthians 3:16).

What an awesome God, who dwells with us and is worthy of our very best—not leftovers or mediocrity, not a hurried lick-and-a-promise effort.

"Whatever you do, do it all for the glory of God." (1 Corinthians 10:31)

PHOTO © Susan Roberts

HORRIBLE, NO-GOOD DAY

Some of you have read the book *Alexander and the Terrible, Horrible, No Good Very Bad Day* to your kids. That was one of our favorites. It is not so funny when it actually happens to you, though. One morning I discovered I had left some frozen blueberries on the counter overnight. The bag had leaked, dripping down the cabinets and onto the floor, staining as it went. I cleaned up the mess and decided to make some banana bread for breakfast. I pulled out a slide-out shelf under my counter to get some sugar, and it broke, sending everything on the shelf spilling onto the floor—sugar, flour and other assorted staples. I cleaned up that mess and turned on the oven, only to realize it wasn't heating. No banana bread. I guess I could have screamed and cussed, but words from a song by Francesca Battistelli ("This is the Stuff that Drives Me Crazy") came to mind and I realized that God was at work in me. Like the song says, God knows what he is doing and uses these hiccups in life to make us stronger and help us learn to trust him.

I laughed. This was not a black cloud day, but a golden day where God was using the stuff of my life to refine my faith. Praise God that he is not finished with us, and cares enough to help us become the person he intended us to be.

> "These have come so that your faith—of greater worth than gold, which perishes even though refined by fire—may be proved genuine and may result in praise, glory and honor when Jesus Christ is revealed." (1 Peter 1:7)

PHOTO © Susan Roberts

WAITING FOR RAIN

My daughter shared with me a YouTube video made by an organization called Onetimeblind. In the skit, the actors join hands and pray for rain then go about their business. One lady returns holding an umbrella. The rest query her, "What are you doing?" She says, "I am waiting for the rain." They tell her to look at the blue, cloudless sky. They say, "It's not going to rain."

Do we have faith to believe God even we see no sign of the answer? That is hard to do. I was inspired by the story of Joshua and the Levite priests who were carrying the ark of the covenant across the Jordan River. The river was rushing at flood stage. The banks were steep and slippery. I'm sure it was a daunting task to maneuver that ark down the embankment and enter the river. God told Joshua to command the priests to step into the water. When their feet touched the water, and not before, God stopped the flow of the river and they crossed on dry land (Joshua 3:15-16).

Catherine Marshall wrote, "There seems to be a point in the application of faith in any problem, when we have to keep pressing forward, in spite of seemingly immovable mountains and no response from God. It is at this time, with no seeming results, when our faith often falters. But when faith persists, it is rewarded by an act of initiative on God's part."[5] Hang in there, and get out your umbrella. Don't be afraid to get your feet wet. God is faithful.

"Now faith is being sure of what we hope for and certain of what we do not see." (Hebrews 11:1)

5. Catherine Marshall, *Moments That Matter* (Nashville: Countryman, 2001).

PHOTO © Larry Lawton

POKING HOLES

Our soil is rock hard, making it difficult for things to grow. Our lawn suffers because we have difficulty getting water and nutrients through the compacted dirt. We watch the weather and try to plan a lawn aeration, just in time for rain. The holes in the ground will let in air and water, and strengthen the grass's roots for more vigorous growth. Without the biannual aeration, our grass would be thin and brown.

It helps to poke holes in our set ways of doing things now and then. This lets in the "water" and "breath" of the Holy Spirit to guide and refresh, to stimulate our "roots" in the Word, and to help us grow in our Christian walk. We become lazy and "thin" in our spirit when we aren't challenged. The resulting lethargy might cause us to miss out on something God has for us, or an opportunity to help and minister. Let's aerate our spirits by opening up to God's work and leading, even if it pokes holes in the way we usually do things.

> "This is what God the Lord says—he who created the heavens, and stretches them out, who spreads out the earth and all that springs out of it, who gives breath to its people, and life to those who walk on it: 'I, the Lord, have called you in righteousness; I will take hold of your hand. I will keep you and will make you to be a covenant for the people and a light for the Gentiles, to open eyes that are blind, to free captives from prison and to release from the dungeon those who sit in darkness.'" (Isaiah 42:5-7)

PHOTO © Susan Roberts

LEARNING FROM WEEDS

You've got to be kidding. How can those persistent plants pop up in such improbable places? I've seen them invading sidewalk cracks and rocks. With the moisture and warm weather, weeds seem to be everywhere and gardeners are preparing to do battle.

You've got to admire those little guys, though! They can be pulled up, stomped on and sprayed with herbicide. They can endure heat, cold and drought. They can be eradicated except for a piece of root. Yet they keep coming back. They are so resilient and tenacious.

We Christians can learn a lot from weeds. We'd probably rather be the delicate flower that gets the *ohhs* and *ahhs*, or the succulent fruit that satisfies the hunger, but neither of these can withstand the elements and abuse. Our society can be pretty hard on Christians—we get stomped on, and efforts may be made to eradicate our principles. We may experience times when we are on the hot seat, or feel coldly snubbed. Our faith may waiver in times of spiritual drought. But if our root remains, firmly established in Jesus' love, we will prevail.

"But blessed is the one who trusts in the Lord, whose confidence is in him. He will be like a tree planted by the water that sends out its roots by the stream. It does not fear when heat comes; its leaves are always green. It has no worries in a year of drought and never fails to bear fruit." (Jeremiah 17:7-8)

PHOTO © Kent Nelson

HERE THEY COME

I watch and wait. I water. Where are they? Will they come? I generally plant a lot of seeds in my garden during the spring. Some come up, some don't. I am trying to figure out if the seeds were bad, if the soil wasn't well-prepared or if they didn't get enough water. I do want to figure out the problem so I can garden successfully.

In 1 Corinthians chapter 3 Paul tells us that we are fellow workers in planting God's seeds of truth or watering what is growing. The early church was often led astray by sin and false teaching, and Paul made every effort to set them on the right course. He did know, however, that though he planted seeds and watered them, it was God who made things grow.

Where might you plant seeds? Do you know people who do not know God? Do you know someone involved in destructive behavior that needs a seed of truth? If you know people who need help, ask God if he is calling you to plant some seeds. Maybe your job is watering a seed already planted. Whatever you do, be cautious and gentle, speaking the truth in love, remembering that it is God who will bring growth. God will prepare their hearts and help you be an effective servant-sower.

"And the Lord's servant must not be quarrelsome: instead he must be kind to everyone, able to teach, not resentful. Those who oppose him he gently instructs, in the hope that God will grant them repentance leading them to a knowledge of the truth, and that they will come to their senses and escape from the trap of the devil, who has taken them captive to do his will." (2 Timothy 2:24-26)

PHOTO © Perry Roberts

IF ONLYS

I feel grumpy. I miss my garden. I have a bad case of the "if onlys." If only our house were built, I could be out planting. This time of year, it seems every store is stocking plants, seeds, and garden supplies—constant reminders of what I cannot do.

I think most of us succumb to the "if onlys" every once in a while. If only my friend or my family hadn't moved away. If only I still had my job. If only the pastor I liked was still here. If only I, or a family member were healthy. If only I didn't have to take care of that problem. If only it was like before. If only, if only, if only, if only. That's a sure way to be disappointed, discontent and grumpy.

Paul wrote that he had learned to be content in every circumstance. Why? Because he could "do everything through him who gives me strength" (Philippians 4:13). How do we receive that strength?

When we look for the hand of God in everything, we will be amazed to see him working, and it is that knowledge that gives us joy. My lack of gardening is giving me time to plant in a new way—seeds of faith, hope and joy as I write. We needn't be stuck in the past with regrets. Change is inevitable. Look ahead with enthusiasm. God may be calling you to something new. You can be confident that he has a good plan, and that he will be faithful. Join me in getting rid of grumpiness, and rejoice in the Lord!

"The joy of the Lord is your strength." (Nehemiah 8:10)

PHOTO © Susan Roberts

BROKEN BRANCHES

Boom! With a crack and a thud, a huge branch crashed to the driveway. The heavy, wet snow was too much of a burden for the trees just sprouting leaves. Even the recommended precautions of brushing away some snow had not been enough. The snow came too quickly and was just too heavy.

The branches of our lives are often overburdened—sometimes quickly and unexpectedly. Even though we take precautions, we might break under the heavy pressure of unexpected problems. What a blessing to know that God will heal the brokenhearted and bind their wounds (*see* Psalm 147:3). When we become broken, we need his help. We can't go it alone. He is there for us. We can cast our burdens on him, because he cares for us (*see* 1 Peter 5:7).

When I read about the repair of broken tree branches, there is not really much that can be done except cleaning away the damaged residue so the tree can start anew. God does that too—helping us get rid of the damage and renewing our spirits within us. He desires us to always come to him humbly, with a contrite spirit, not putting our trust in other things, but in him alone (*see* Psalm 147:10-11). Then he can help us. In him is strength, hope, peace and salvation.

"The Lord is close to the brokenhearted and saves those who are crushed in spirit. A righteous man may have many troubles, but the Lord delivers him from them all." (Psalm 34:18-19)

PHOTO © Susan Roberts

A TIP FOR YOU

Shows on the TV cooking channel offer tips for grilling. Did you know hamburger patties cook better if you shape a shallow well in the center, and chicken breasts cook more evenly if you pound them slightly to a uniform thickness? Similarly, the attendants at our local greenhouse give me tips. For instance, seeds germinate better if soaked in water for 24 hours prior to planting. Dawn dishwashing liquid diluted in water makes a great spray for aphids and mites. Learning new things motivates me to get going on my gardening or grilling. I am anxious to see if these tips work.

Reading God's Word has a similar effect. When I learn tips about how God works and Who he is, it inspires me to live in accordance with his directives to see if it works. As I have been reading through the Old Testament, I see God's dealings with the nation of Israel. It has been reiterated over and over again how important obedience is to God. He wants us to follow his directives unconditionally—not so we can be squelched in our freedom, but so he can bless us. He told the people that he was giving them the choice of a blessed life or a cursed one, based on whether they decided to obey him or not. Paul tells us in Romans that we are free from sin, but slaves to righteousness (*see* Romans 6:18). God loves us so much that he knows what works best for us. Be inspired to follow his advice. It works!

> "Listen to my instruction and be wise....Blessed are those who listen to me, watching daily at my doors, waiting at my doorway." (Proverbs 8:33-34)

PHOTO © Pat Burdick

THE RABBIT AND BEANS

It was bean planting time. I was stooping over the raised bed, placing bedding plants in holes, when a rabbit came within a few feet of me. Explaining garden etiquette, I patiently informed him my bean plants were not his to nibble, but he could enjoy the grass or other delectables in my yard that would not be destroyed by his feasting. He proceeded, however, to chomp on my baby bean plants right in front of me! I promptly shooed this critter from my garden!

God has set out rules for us too. his first rule began with Adam and Eve. He told them not to eat of a certain tree in his garden. They chomped on the fruit anyway. He shooed them out of his garden. Unlike my rabbit, they perfectly understood his directive, but they disobeyed. We may think that God's rules are an imposition on happiness, satisfaction and freedom. But God's rules are for our benefit. David outlined the benefits of God's laws in Psalm 19. They revive us, make us wise, and show us truth about who God is. They warn us of pitfalls. Keeping them brings us great reward and blessing. Paul adds in Romans 6 that the benefit of lawfulness is holiness leading to eternal life. Most of all, God's law shows us our sinful nature and our inability to be righteous on our own. We need a Savior. We need grace that protects us from ourselves and allows us to be something we can't be by ourselves. Jesus' sacrifice for us allows us to be welcomed back into God's garden where we can "taste and see that the Lord is good" (Psalm 34:8).

"For all have sinned and fall short of the glory of God, and are justified freely by his grace through the redemption that came by Jesus Christ." (Romans 3:23-24)

PHOTO © CanStockPhoto Inc / Elenathewise

SPRINGING UP

I love to see this new season spring up. My favorite pop-ups are the narcissus—also known as jonquil and daffodil. I read that there are over sixty varieties from white to yellows to orange, in several sizes and shapes.

The name *narcissus* is said to come from the myth about the handsome young man named Narcissus, who saw his reflection in a pool of water. He was so enamored with his own image that he stared for several hours. Eventually, he fell asleep and toppled into the pool and drowned. The pretty narcissus flowers are said to have grown in the place where he died. his self-love was his undoing.

I am intrigued by the contrast between Eli's sons' self-centeredness and Hannah's selflessness in 1 Samuel chapters 1 and 2. Eli's sons Hophni and Phinehas selfishly took the choicest parts of the sacrificial meat for themselves, roasting it instead of boiling it as God had commanded. Hannah, on the other hand, selflessly gave her only son to God's service. God blessed Samuel and Hannah, but Hophni and Phinehas's selfishness was their undoing. We live in a world that teaches us to focus on ourselves—the "me" generation. That is not what God desires.

Look at your reflection. What do you see? Are you self-absorbed like Narcissus, or do you deny yourself and pursue God? Consider the consequences.

"Turn my heart toward your statutes and not toward selfish gain. Turn my eyes away from worthless things; preserve my life according to your word."
(Psalm 119:36-37)

PHOTO © Perry Roberts

WHAT DO YOU DO WITH DANDELIONS?

Did you know you can eat dandelions? Not long ago, when we were on a tour, the guide picked some of the flowers and ate them, remarking how flavorful they were and how great they could be in salads. There is also dandelion wine, dandelion tea and even weight loss applications from the roots. I remember picking bouquets of dandelions when I was a little girl, and joyfully bringing them to my Mom. Who hasn't had the fun of blowing the puff balls when the flowers go to seed? But, in most yards, dandelions are not welcome. Instead, we get out the Weed and Feed® and rid our lawns of this pesky, unwanted intrusion.

Lots of things are a matter of perspective. When we attend church, we may be delighted or disappointed by the choice of songs, the components of the service, the sermon topic or the overall appearance of the sanctuary. How easy it is to be critical and walk out grumbling when things are not to our liking. However, the things that may not minister to us personally may be just what someone else needs to lighten their spirit and open their heart to God's voice. When you do not feel a special connection, remember, it is a matter of perspective. You may think of these things as weeds in the service, but they may bring nourishment to someone else. Pray a blessing for someone else.

"Do nothing out of selfish ambition or vain conceit, but in humility consider others better than yourselves, not looking to your own interests but each of you to the interests of others." (Philippians 2:3-4, NIVUK)

PHOTO © Susan Roberts

GETTING TO KNOW YOU

We were in a small group study with some couples we did not know very well. Over several years we learned more about them—their ideas, their theology, and their concerns as we prayed together. There was little time to visit, though, as we stuck to our schedule. My husband and I decided it was time to get to know these people better. We invited one couple out to dinner and learned more about them in that short time than we had in years of our small group meetings. Really knowing someone is an important part of connecting with them. It takes time and effort. But it is worth it.

Knowing God is even more important. If we don't know God's character, how can we trust him? If don't understand how big he is, how can we be assured that he is able to address our problems? If we don't understand his love, how can we be confident that he will care for us, and not harm us? How can we take hold of his wonderful gifts and promises if we don't know what they are? How can we effectively serve him if we don't know what pleases or displeases him?

Getting to know God is also worth the effort. When we read his Word, spend time talking and listening to him in prayer, pay attention and observe him at work, we are empowered and our spirits are settled with peace.

"I keep asking that the God of our Lord Jesus Christ, the glorious Father, may give you the Spirit of wisdom and revelation, so that you may know him better. I pray also that the eyes of your heart may be enlightened in order that you may know the hope to which he has called you, the riches of his glorious inheritance to the saints, and his incomparably great power for us who believe." (Ephesians 1:17-19)

PHOTO © Chris Roberts

DANCING IN THE RAIN

The rain came in sheets, the thunder boomed, and lightning flashed. We were glad to be safe inside the house. It seemed to stop so we went to the store. Then later, as we exited the store, another squall soaked us as we hurried to our car.

This reminded me of a visit to a friend's home in Brighton last summer. Just as we arrived, the skies opened up and it poured. We waited a while in the car, but the rain didn't let up. We were annoyed at the delay. Finally, we knew we would have to brave the deluge if we were to get inside. We hustled as quickly as we could (and we not do move all that quickly) to the shelter of our friend's home. As we shook off the wet in their entry way, we noticed a sign on their wall and had to laugh. It read, "Life is not about weathering the storms, but learning to dance in the rain." Maybe we should have entered the house a bit differently. Perhaps we need to do a little more dancing.

Trials will actually be beneficial to us if we let them. Not all days are sunny. Not all of our exploits go smoothly. We can be grouchy about the circumstances and do all we can to avoid them. Or, we can make the best of our situation and do some dancing.

"Consider it pure joy, my brothers, whenever you face trials of many kinds."
(James 1:2)

PHOTO © Chris Adams

PLAYHOUSE DISCIPLINE

My husband's sister was a jabber box in school. Her kindergarten teacher attempted to correct this behavior by removing her from the temptation and placing her by herself in time out. The time-out corner was a playhouse. She loved being there, so she invented ways to get in trouble. It took the teacher a while to learn that this was not an effective punishment.

We had an interesting discussion in our small group about ways we were disciplined as children, and ways we disciplined our own children. Despite the method, we all agreed that discipline is very important to training, character formation, safety and ultimately, happiness. We discipline our children out of love and concern for them. As we have read through Leviticus, we see how God has given laws and disciplined the children of Israel when they failed to obey him. God disciplines us because he loves us. Though it is not pleasant, it is effective and just what we need, because he knows us.

"My son, do not make light of the Lord's discipline, and do not lose heart when he rebukes you, because the Lord disciplines those he loves, and punishes everyone he accepts as his son....Moreover, we have all had human fathers who disciplined us and we respected them for it. How much more should we submit to the Father of our spirits and live! Our fathers disciplined us for a little while as they thought best; but God disciplines us for our good, that we may share in his holiness." (Hebrews 12:5-10)

PHOTO © Carol Cassell

ON THE TEAM

All our kids played soccer. Although my husband and I sometimes refereed or coached, our primary role was spectator. We cheered and encouraged, yelled at the ref, criticized the coach, and engaged in "should haves" and "whys." Our kids, on the other hand, were passionately involved in the sport as players. They did spend time on the bench, particularly when injured, but they remained ready to play—warming up and paying close attention to the coach's instructions. On the field, they eagerly participated in the plays, working through pain and fatigue. They practiced daily. Sometimes the coach disappointed them by assigning them to a position they'd rather not play, but they stepped up to the task. They did what it took to win.

As believers, we are all on God's team. We are not supposed to just be spectators—analyzing, criticizing, and second guessing. God, our coach, may sit us on the bench to heal or wait. We may experience seasons of preparation and practice. Other times we enthusiastically join the game, using our best efforts and talents to help our team win. We may even be assigned to a role we'd rather not play, but we listen and do what it takes to help our team.

Get up, get out there, give it your all, You are on the winning side.

"Strip down, start running—and never quit! No extra spiritual fat, no parasitic sins. Keep your eyes on Jesus. Study how he did it....He could put up with anything along the way: Cross, shame, whatever....When you find yourselves flagging in your faith, go over that story again...That will shoot adrenaline into your souls!" (Hebrews 12:1-2, The Message)

PHOTOS © Susan Roberts

JELLY BEANS

Our grandsons got the giggles when they realized that the Star Wars jelly beans we had given them stained their tongues blue. They kept running to the mirror to check their tongues. They loved posing for pictures with their blue tongues sticking out. Their Mom didn't like the thought of them going to school the next day with blue tongues and lips. She was happy that the stain only lasted a short time and was easily removed with toothpaste.

Stains are not something we view as positive. Stains on fabrics, walls, floors, or body parts usually cause a concentrated cleaning effort. Sometimes it is successful, sometimes not. Sin in our lives also leaves a stain and breaks our fellowship with a holy God. "Although you wash yourself with soap and use an abundance of cleansing powder, the stain of your guilt is still before me, declares the Sovereign Lord" (Jeremiah 2:22).

But God in his love provided a way to wash away the stain of our sin, not with soap or toothpaste, but with Jesus' blood. Aren't you glad that through the grace of the Lord we all have access to the ultimate stain remover? It always works. Praise God.

"Christ loved the church and gave himself up for her to make her holy, cleansing her by the washing with water through the word, and to present her to himself as a radiant church, without stain or wrinkle or any other blemish, but holy and blameless." (Ephesians 5:25-27)

PHOTO © Chris Roberts

SOARING

I held the stick gingerly, careful not to move it too much. I slowly pulled it toward me, then tipped it carefully to the right. I was afraid to make bold movements. This was my reaction to trying to fly a plane when my son took me up in a Cessna. He had done this so much that he felt confident and calm. When he had the yoke, or control column, he banked the plane nearly vertical, swooping in a circle. I was quite the opposite. Gradually, though, I became more confident and actually enjoyed the challenge.

John A. Shedd said, "A ship is always safe at the shore, but that is not what it is built for." Same with a plane: flying always involves risk, especially for someone without training and experience. But planes are built for soaring.

Francis Chan has conducted seminars on Christian risk taking. (Check out his balance beam video on YouTube). We often seek security. We find it hard to walk by faith and step out in courage to try something new. We might think we lack the necessary skills or training. We might be afraid of failure. Remaining an observer is far easier but not what God "built" us for. God intends for us to soar. He created humankind in his image with unimaginable resources through him. Let us awaken our hearts and listen to his call, then step out in faith. Yes, we might fail; but the lessons learned can help us come back bigger and bolder the next time. He wants to train us and teach us, so that we will be confident, mature and complete, not lacking anything (*see* James 1:4).

"Be strong and courageous. Do not be terrified; do not be discouraged, for the Lord your God will be with you wherever you go." (Joshua 1:9)

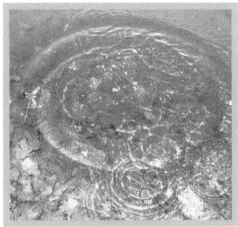

PHOTO © Susan Roberts

RIPPLES

Kerplunk! The rock splashed into the creek amidst the giggles of our grandkids. The biggest rocks made the best splash, but even the littlest ones disturbed the surface and sent rings in ever widening circles. We stood on the bridge above the sluggish water and dropped rocks to the surface below. Each time we threw a rock, we purposefully waited until the water was still again so we could see the splash and resulting ripples.

When we take action, whether it is big or little, it has an impact on those around us. Perhaps it is negative. Perhaps it is positive. A careless word or action can cause anger and a compromised self image. Kind words and thoughtful deeds can be healing and empowering. Our choices can have a ripple effect that spreads wider than we might think. Even a simple smile can bring a wave of joy as people "Pay it forward." On the other hand, a hateful look can be devastating.

A man drove his car in the drive-through at Starbucks. When he paid for his coffee, as a random act of kindness, he also paid for the car behind him. This started a chain reaction that brought good will and a cup of coffee to hundreds of people that day. Who would've thought this simple act could have had such a far-reaching effect?

Purposefully make sure that the ripples you send out are positive ones. You never know how far they'll go.

"Whatever you do, whether in word or deed, do it all in the name of the Lord Jesus." (Colossians 3:17)

PHOTO © Kent Nelson

BRIDGE OVER TROUBLED WATER

Lately, my husband and I have found ourselves placed in the awkward position of running interference for folks in the midst of interpersonal conflict. They have their own agenda and stick to it tenaciously. They have put up walls that prevent them from hearing and understanding the other's point of view. Our advice has been to let words and actions build bridges instead of walls. The Simon and Garfunkel song, "Bridge Over Troubled Water" comes to mind.

> "I'll take your part when darkness comes and pain is all around
> Like a bridge over troubled water I will lay me down."

Relationships are not always about being right, holding your ground, and making yourself heard. "Lay yourself down" by putting aside your own agenda to help another.

Love, forgiveness, kindness, acceptance and humility are all building blocks that help make bridges. Anger, pride, selfishness, judging and grudges build walls. We are all Christians under construction, and we make mistakes. But, let us work to build more bridges than walls. Paul says that he put aside his own knowledge and freedom for the sake of others.

"I have become all things to all men so that by all possible means I might save some." (1 Corinthians 9:22b)

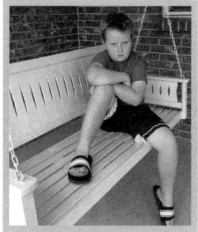

PHOTO © Susan Roberts

MY PORCH SWING

One afternoon a family with small children came to visit us. The young boy sat defiantly on our front porch swing, while the girls begged him for a turn. He was in an obstinate mood and would not budge. In frustration, the girls came into the kitchen to tattle. I was making cookies. The girls were soon eagerly helping me bake, the swing forgotten. About the time the cookies came out of the oven, the boy, bored by the lack of attention, came into the house. He wanted a cookie. I told him that that was up to the bakers. Since he had been so mean to them, they had the right to choose to share or not. They could repay his unkindness with more unkindness, or they could be forgiving. The girls, proud of their accomplishment, graciously and enthusiastically shared their cookies with him.

This little boy received something he did not deserve…grace. We, too, are always receiving what we do not deserve—God's unmerited favor: abundant grace. All of us have sinned and deserve punishment. We should be treated according to our behavior. But God is not like that. He forgives us and removes our transgressions from us. his love is so great that he not only treats us with grace, but he gives us wonderful gifts, and adopts us into his family as his beloved children. So take, eat. This is amazing grace.

"He does not treat us as our sins deserve or repay us according to our iniquities." (Psalm 103:10)

THE COCK CROWED

In the early morning mist a rooster crowed. The chill that ran through Peter was not from the dew and cool morning breeze. He was overcome with grief, regret, and embarrassment. He had denied his Master three times. He wept.

How like Peter we are. We fail to make a stand for Jesus in the workplace, our homes, and our neighborhoods. It is too easy to follow the crowd, not stand out, not make waves, not wanting to be associated with "those religious weirdos." Later, we experience grief, regret, and remorse. Our failure to speak and act, our safe words, are equivalent to Peter's: "I never knew him."

So what made the difference in Peter? Even after it was confirmed Jesus had risen, the disciples remained in hiding, fearful. As political and religious tensions continued, aligning themselves with Jesus was not a wise move. A short time later, however, we see Peter boldly preaching (*see* Acts 2:14). Peter's transformation begins with Jesus' forgiveness and love in spite of his failures, then continues with empowering by the Holy Spirit.

The book of Acts begins with the disciples and early Christians receiving the promised gift of the Holy Spirit. Jesus had told them that he would send his Spirit to comfort them, convict of sin, and lead them to truth (*see* John chapters 14 and 16). But they also received power. As we seek to stand up for Jesus in a decaying world, let us draw from his love, forgiveness, truth and power so that we are transformed from our reluctant selves to Spirit-filled believers who will stand up boldly, carrying his message to a world in need.

"And you will receive power." (Acts 1:8)

PHOTO © Susan Roberts

PIERCED BY A THORN

Thanks to great spring weather, I took time to begin garden cleanup. I raked leaves and cleared away dead debris, preparing for new sprouts and seeds. I laid down new mulch. While pruning rose bushes, I was inadvertently pierced by a sharp thorn. Botanists say this was only a prickle, not a thorn. But, *ouch!* Just that tiny hole in my finger caused me discomfort for the rest of the day.

As I have pondered the events of Easter week, I have thought about the crown of thorns placed on Jesus' brow (see Matthew 27:28-29). Although the precise type of thorn bush used isn't known, the thorns were most certainly much bigger and sharper than those of my rose bush. I cannot even imagine the pain. What Jesus endured for our sin is unfathomable! I read about a creative way to celebrate Easter: have a bonfire on Good Friday. Each person throws a ring made of thorn branches onto the fire as a reminder of the suffering Jesus endured, but also as a reminder that his loving act completely destroyed the power of our sin forever.

In the horrendous events of Good Friday, our Savior suffered and died. But Easter brought an incredible event. Jesus rose again, claiming victory over sin and death. It is finished. Praise God! The victory is ours.

> "But he was pierced for our transgressions, he was crushed for our iniquities; the punishment that brought us peace was upon him, and by his wounds we are healed." (Isaiah 53:5)

PHOTO © Chris Roberts

PHOTO © Dr. John Dennehy

WHO'S CALLING?

An eerie howl pierced the quiet of the evening. My husband and I looked at each other and said simultaneously, "What was that?" We heard a sound like a scream or a wail. A little research showed us that it was a fox call. Yes, we now know what the fox says. Our research also showed that each family of foxes has a distinct voice, recognizable by the others. Varying tones represent their communication, usually initiated by the mom. She calls them to dinner, she "interrogates" them to see where they are and what they are doing, and she alerts them to danger.

When I was growing up in the days before cell phones, our neighborhood moms had varied calls too. My mom used a large bell, another had a whistle, and a third a horn. We were to stay within range and pay attention. When we heard our call, we were to drop what we were doing and run home.

God calls us as well, and we should be attentive to his voice. Listen to what God is calling you to do. Some of us are called to ministries and fulltime service. Some are called to be leaders or organizers. Many are called to be a quiet light in a dark place. There is no greater call than parenting. We are so grateful to all the Moms out there who not only hear God's call but take on the role of caring for their "pack." Thank you.

> "We constantly pray for you, that our God may count you worthy of his calling, and that by his power he may fulfill every good purpose of yours and every act prompted by your faith." (2 Thessalonians 1:11)

PHOTO © Susan Roberts

THANKS, VETS

It was silent in the St. Louis Soccer Arena. Several thousand people listened intently to the ceremony. Then a roar erupted. Goalkeeper and fan favorite, Slobodan Illejevski, had become a US citizen. I still remember the tears in his eyes as he embraced his new country.

Slobo grew up in Yugoslavia, very poor. He rarely had access to soccer balls, so he used rolled-up rags or even rocks when he played in the streets. Yet, he had such a positive attitude, with no complaints. He quipped, "You be one tough goalie, you play soccer with rocks."

his appreciation of America had a profound impact on me. Often we do not appreciate all that we have. We live in a beautiful land that provides freedom of speech, freedom to vote, freedom to bear arms, freedom to worship as we choose, and freedom to follow our dreams. Most places in the world do not offer these benefits.

Yet many of us complain. This country has problems, but it also has greatness. Let us choose to focus on the good, grateful for what we have.

Men and women in the military sacrifice to serve the USA and strive to preserve these freedoms that we often take for granted. Many have given their lives so that we can enjoy these freedoms. We give them our heartfelt thanks. Commit to pray for our country's future and the safety of our service people. God bless America.

"Be joyful always; pray continually; give thanks in all circumstances, for this is God's will for you in Christ Jesus." (1 Thessalonians 5:16-18)

SUMMER

PHOTO © Susan Roberts

LIKE A ROCK

This balanced rock is pretty impressive. How in the world does it continue to stand? In places like Garden of the Gods in Colorado Springs and Arches National Park in Utah, huge boulders perch precariously on slender columns, causing us to shake our heads in disbelief. Why have they not toppled with the passage of time? Perhaps someday they will. Solid rock, no matter how stable it appears, is not imperious to the elements. Wind, water, storms and time take their toll, cracking, shaping, carving and breaking down their sturdiness. The instability and the threat of rock slides remind us that we must be careful, and not place our confidence in these seemingly solid structures.

When David tells us to trust God as our solid rock, we can be assured God will not change over time (*see* Hebrews 13:8) or be corrupted by outside influences. He will not tumble, fall, or crack under pressure. He never sleeps. Other forms of security are unreliable. "No king is saved by the size of his army; no warrior escapes with great strength. A horse is a vain hope for deliverance; despite all its strength it cannot save" (Psalm 33:16-17). How awesome it is to know we can count on God whatever the circumstances. When the storms of life come, don't trust in the things that are solid and strong in appearance only. Trust in the one who is truly able to help.

"For who is God besides the Lord? And who is the Rock except our God? It is God who arms me with strength and keeps my way secure." (Psalm 18:31-32, NIVUK)

PHOTO © Susan Roberts

JOSHUA TREES

In the southwest deserts there is a tree (really more of a yucca or cactus), called the Joshua Tree. We visited Joshua Tree National Park in southern California and learned that these trees were named by early travelers enduring the hardships of crossing the arid deserts in that area. They thought the trees looked like Joshua, pointing the way to the Promised Land. The Bible tells us that Joshua and Caleb were the only two spies who had faith that God would overcome the obstacles that lay ahead. Unlike the other Israelites, they did not complain or feel defeated by the challenges. Through their leadership, the Israelites eventually found rest and refreshment.

This story was an encouragement to American pioneers of westward expansion who were in the midst of a difficult journey. When they saw trees in the desert, they remembered to trust God to get them through the difficulties to their own "promised land."

In our life travels, we also experience "deserts" or times of "drought" when hope and promises seem out of reach. It is easy to become discouraged and want to give up or give in. It is important to stay attuned to the stories in God's Word, and remember his past faithfulness, to be strengthened and our spirits and encouraged in our walk.

"Let the hearts of those who seek the Lord rejoice. Look to the Lord and his strength; seek his face always. Remember the wonders he has done..."
(1 Chronicles 16:9-11)

PHOTO © Susan Roberts

WATERFALLS

On a trip through several western states we visited many beautiful waterfalls: Twin Falls and Shoshone Falls in Idaho; several exquisite falls along the Columbia River Gorge that we hiked right up to, felt the spray, and walked beneath. Glacier National Park has waterfalls everywhere. Some even cascade onto the road, and many stream down from great heights over several different levels. We also saw waterfalls in Yellowstone National Park. The one pictured above is Shannon Falls near Vancouver, BC. We love the uniqueness and magnificence of each fall—and of course we took lots of pictures!

Chris Tomlin wrote a song called "Waterfall," which is a metaphor for the outpouring of God's love. In an interview he gave on KLOVE radio shortly after the song was released, Chris said his inspiration was from Isaiah 41:18: "I will make rivers flow from barren heights, and springs within the valleys. I will turn the desert into pools of water, and the parched ground into springs." God pours out his love like a waterfall on our parched and dry spirits. The cool water refreshes our innermost being and helps us spring into life. Chris also found inspiration in Psalm 42:1: "As a deer pants for streams of water, so my soul pants for you, my God." Only God can satisfy our deepest longings. He does not disappoint. Surely his love is beautiful, like a waterfall—poured out to us unconditionally, without ceasing.

"And hope does not disappoint us, because God's has poured out his love into our hearts by the Holy Spirit, whom he has given us." (Romans 5:5)

PHOTO © CanStockPhoto Inc / svanhorn

START YOUR JOURNEY

Although our car has GPS, we still like to bring our huge atlas when we travel. The GPS decides on a route, but we check it on the printed map. Sometimes we follow what the GPS tells us to do. Sometimes we choose our own way. The GPS might want us to go on a toll road, and we would like to avoid the fees. There might be points of interest on another route that we would like to see. At times we even have additional information, like road construction, so we choose an alternative road.

It doesn't matter how you get there. Start the journey. There is some truth in this. Starting our journey to our eternal home in heaven, by accepting Jesus' grace and believing in his love and sacrifice for us is the most important decision we can make. Start your journey! And, yes, we all have different ways of getting there. We have different gifts and ministries. Our lives lead us through different paths and challenges. But God says there is only one way to him and eternal life (see John 14:6). We cannot follow our own ideas and plans. We need to follow Jesus. We cannot develop our own standard of morality. God's truth and laws are absolute. We cannot travel by our own strength and initiative. Our good works do not earn us a place in heaven. We need him—the gift of his grace. So, get going on your journey, but take the narrow road, the right road. Follow the path the God has laid out for you, not turning to the right or left. Keep your eternal destination in sight.

> "Wide is the gate and broad is the road that leads to destruction, and many enter through it. But small is the gate and narrow the road that leads to life, and only a few find it." (Matthew 7:13-14)

PHOTO © Dr. John Dennehy

INTO THE HARBOR

We love the beautiful drive along the Oregon coast. Numerous lighthouses staccato the rocks, and we couldn't help but stop. We learned that lighthouse keepers of the past had to be very careful to keep the fires burning in the tower, and to keep the lens and window clean so that the light could shine and guide ships past dangers into the safety of the harbor. A special lens called a Fresnel was eventually developed to focus and amplify the light so it could be seen twenty-four miles out to sea. Many sailors have told stories of their relief upon seeing the harbor light in the midst of a storm as they returned from an arduous journey.

Jesus said, "You are the light of the world" (Matthew 5:14). We are to let our light shine and not hide it. We are to reflect and refocus the true light of Jesus. We don't produce light on our own; we are merely the lens that is amplifying his light for the world to see.

How do we keep our light shining brightly?

- By abiding in his light so we can reflect his light (*see* I John 1:7).
- By relying on Jesus' forgiveness and cleansing to keep our lens clean (see 1 John 1:9).
- By humbling ourselves and trusting the Lord to lift us to a place where we will be seen by those in need, and where we can be most effective in guiding people to him (*see* James 4:10).

"Let your light so shine before men, that they may see your good deeds and praise your Father in heaven." (Matthew 5:16)

PHOTO © Jana Osterlund

BUGS ON THE WINDOW

If you have driven on the freeway in the summertime, you have probably experienced "bug plaster." Numerous little bugs splat against the windshield, but it is the big gross one that makes us stop at the next gas station. Windshield wipers and washer fluid merely smear the mess, so a good window washing is necessary. A rain storm can give relief, but usually even that is not sufficient. Nothing works as well as a thorough scrubbing.

We heard a song on the radio with the lyric "It's a beautiful day, but I wouldn't mind some rain to wash the bugs off my window." The song talks about how, as we go along, little hassles of life, interruptions and busyness cloud our vision. A big mess sends us to our knees for immediate results; but over time, little splatters collect almost imperceptibly and obscure our way. Storms can clear away the unimportant pursuits and sharpen our focus on what matters. Problems have a way of putting the stuff of life into perspective; but they don't complete the job. We still need to stop frequently and be washed. That is precisely what Jesus does. his blood washes us from the mess of guilt and sin. Then we are clean.

> "Christ loved the church and gave himself up for her to make her holy, cleansing her by the washing with water through the word, and to present her to himself as a radiant church, without stain or wrinkle or any other blemish, but holy and blameless." (Ephesians 5:25-27)

PHOTO © Eileen Maetzer

RV TRIP

Oh no. Grab the wheel and steer to the side of the road. The vehicle could barely be controlled, but the experienced driver maneuvered it safely to the shoulder of the highway. Friends of ours, traveling in their RV, had a blowout. They were in the middle of nowhere. With no nearby towns and no cell service, they had to change the tire themselves. Thankfully, they were able to put on the spare and limp to a town for a replacement tire.

Kevin Kendrick, the director of the movie *War Room* said, "Prayer is not a spare tire that we pull out when we need it—it's the steering wheel."[6] The flat tire caused momentary difficulty, but even more devastating is neglecting to steer.

Who is controlling your vehicle? Have you left it up to chance? Are you trying desperately to maneuver yourself though emergencies, praying for help only when you find yourself falling flat? Prayer is not just for quick fixes. God is the experienced driver who can steer us over bumps and flats, helping us arrive safely.

> "Trust in the Lord with all your heart and lean not on your own understanding,
> In all your ways acknowledge him and he shall direct your paths."
> (Proverbs 3:5-6, NKJV)

6. Kevin Porter, "'War Room Director: 'Prayer Is Not a Spare Tire, It's the Steering Wheel'," *Christian Post Reporter*, Aug. 28, 2015. Accessed 10-26-2016 at: http://www.christianpost.com/news/war-room-director-prayer-is-not-a-spare-tire-its-the-steering-wheel-143780/

PHOTO © Perry Roberts

A GOOD CATCH

Fisherman know that some days you catch your limit, but other days you don't. My family went on a fishing trip in Alaska. This time they caught a lot of fish—my niece, particularly, had success. As the crew hung their fish on the pier for filleting, we learned that two other people on the boat had not been as successful. After fishing several hours, the group had landed two fish.

Jesus' disciples had fished all night and caught nothing. As the sun rose, they returned to shore despondent. Jesus said, "Try the other side of the boat."

"What? We've fished all night and there was nothing. How can fishing on the other side of the boat make a difference?" they wondered. But they obeyed—and caught more fish than their nets could hold (see John 21:6). That is the power and authority of Jesus!

At times I have tried my best to be a fisher of men but haven't brought a single person to the Lord. That's the point. My best logic and knowledge couldn't accomplish it. When I force the issue, I can actually offend people and turn them away from God, badgering them with my proselytizing. Rick Warren comments in *The Purpose Driven Life*[7] that instead of asking God to come alongside us in what we are doing, we need to join him in what he is doing. Then our work for the Lord will bear fruit. Don't expend all you energy fishing all night for nothing. Follow what the master says. Maybe you need to try the other side of the boat.

"No one can come to me unless the Father who sent me draws him." (John 6:44)

7. Rick Warren, *The Purpose Driven Life* (Zondervan: 2012).

PHOTO © Perry Roberts

GEMS ARE IN HERE SOMEWHERE

I sifted through the gravel looking for that clear sparkling stone. I had purchased a bucket of ordinary-looking gravel at a sapphire mine in Montana. I washed it, swished it around on a screen in the sluice, and then dumped it on a rough wooden table. The water washes away the dirt, and the swishing causes the sapphires, which are heavier than the gravel, to settle to the bottom of the screen. When it is dumped over, sapphires glisten on the top. I sifted through the gravel a few more times to make sure I didn't miss any.

In my read-through-the-Bible program, I dreaded going through Leviticus and Numbers with their boring lists, names, and laws. I found, though, that reading these Old Testament books is like sapphire hunting. One must sift through a lot of ordinary, colorless gravel. But diligent searching reveals valuable gems that show who God is—his righteousness, holiness, and order—and what pleases him. Here's one I found: "The Lord is slow to anger and abounding in love and forgiving of sin and rebellion. Yet he does not leave the guilty unpunished" (Numbers 14:18).

As you read through more difficult passages of scripture, don't just skim through to get it done. Search for the gems. Solomon challenges us to embark on a quest to find the valuable truths in God's Word:

> "My son, if you accept my words and store up my commands within you, turning your ear to wisdom and applying your heart to understanding, and if you call out for insight and cry aloud for understanding, and if you look for it as for silver and search for it as for hidden treasure, then you will understand the fear of the Lord." (Proverbs 2:1-5)

PHOTO © Lisa Carlson

FRUIT-PACKING PLANT

Trucks full of peaches pulled up to the processing plant where they were unloaded. The fruit was washed in huge vats and sent to conveyor belts. We were amazed at the precision and detail used to process each peach. Stickers were applied to indicate the date, location and picker of each piece. The owner, our tour guide, explained how different sizes and qualities of fruit were sorted and directed to different places to either be packaged, boxed, or discarded as "culls." He told us the fruit that was large and perfect in form and color was most valued by consumers, bringing the best market price. However, appearances are deceiving. Farmers know the mottled, smaller pieces actually taste better.

We tend to favor the more attractive people too. Hollywood touts the "beautiful people," but we have all seen they are not especially admirable in their behavior. When God chose David to be king, Samuel was surprised that God didn't choose David's older, taller and more handsome brother. God was more interested in David's character than he was in Abinadab's looks. Many of us spend a lot of time and money on our outward appearances. Perhaps we should send more time "primping" our heart appearance for God. Our inner sweetness, not our good looks, is what pleases God. Let us pray that our hearts become more beautiful. Let us also endeavor to see others, not by the way they look on the outside, but through God's eyes."

"I pray that out of his glorious riches he may strengthen you with power through his Spirit in your inner being." (Ephesians 3:16)

PHOTO © Susan Roberts

GAS MASKS

The soldiers exited the building gasping and coughing. They stumbled, barely able to see. Those waiting were filled with trepidation. They were next. When my husband was in the military, he had to go through specialized training with a gas mask. Each soldier in the unit put on a mask and made sure it fit properly and was secure. Then they walked into a tent or building. They exercised to stir up the dust that had settled. All was fine until they were told to remove their masks. Immediately they couldn't breathe and their eyes watered so much that they could not see. The CS gas was potent. After only a few seconds, they quickly vacated the building and, in relief, gulped the fresh air outside. The oxygen restored their burning lungs.

I heard Levi Lusko speak on the radio while he was on a tour called "O2." He commented that the pollution of sin is very thick around us. We can't breathe. We can't see our way. Life can be sucked out of our spiritual wellbeing. Like the soldiers without gas masks whose bodies require oxygen, our spirits require God. He is our protection and filter. He is not a "nice to have" but an absolute necessity. When we go to him and read his Word and spend time with him, he breathes life into our spirit and we receive the protection we need to handle the toxic world around us.

"The Spirit of God has made me; the breath of the Almighty gives me life."
(Job 33:4)

PHOTO © Mike Kepto

GETTING A TICKET

Flashing lights behind my car always start my heart pounding. Yup, I was being pulled over. The officer asked if I knew why he had stopped me. I wasn't speeding, so I told him I had no clue. He explained that I had failed to use a turn signal when I merged into a right turn lane, and had waited too long before turning right. *You're kidding me!* I thought. But I got a ticket.

Soon after this experience, I learned that across the country hundreds of new laws began on January 1, 2016.[8] How can a person be aware of them all?

God's Old Testament laws were pretty picky, too. There was so much to remember, and failure to know the law was not an excuse. In fact, James tells us that even knowing the right thing to do and not doing it is a violation and doing everything right, yet failing in one point, is still cause for penalty (*see* James 2:10; 4:17). The penalty for breaking God's law is pretty stiff: death (at least I just got a ticket!). How thankful we are for grace! Incredibly, God will use us for his purposes and extend his call to us even as sinful and imperfect as we are. We don't need to clean up first. We just need to be willing.

> *"We aren't saved from sin's grasp by knowing the commandments of God because we can't and don't keep them, but God put into effect a different plan to save us. He sent his own Son in a human body like ours—except that ours are sinful—and destroyed sin's control over us by giving himself as a sacrifice for our sins. So now we can obey God's laws if we follow after the Holy Spirit and no longer obey the old evil nature within us."* (Romans 8:3-4, TLB)

8. Pete Williams, "New Year's Day: Hundreds of Laws Across the Country Go into Effect," *US News* (January 1, 2016).

PHOTO © Jana Osterlund

AWESOME GOD

Travels opens new vistas to the beauty of God's creation. We love seeing critters on our travels : starfish, crabs and sand dollars at beach; whales and dolphins in the ocean; and bears, bison, bighorn sheep, mountain goats and moose in the mountains and forests. We marvel at the scenery—rocky cliffs, waterfalls, lava flows, spouting geysers and snowcapped mountain peaks. We enjoy beautiful sunrises and sunsets. At one point, when visiting Glacier National Park in Montana, we couldn't help but break into a chorus of "How Great Thou Art." The Bible says that if we don't praise God, even the stones will cry out in worship (*see* Luke 11:40).

Returning home, we were reminded that God's handiwork is everywhere. We don't need to travel to see it. God's fingerprint is all around us, right where we are. We just need to take a moment to notice. We gasp at stunning sunrises and sunsets. We smile when we see baby foxes playing in our back yard. We delight in early-morning bird chorus. Beautiful roses bloom in our front yard and even the tiny bug crawling up our sidewalk is amazing. When God created the world, he saw that it was good. I'm sure he smiled. How wonderful to realize that all this was not just created for God's enjoyment, but for ours. He is delighted when we appreciate what he has made for us.

"Come and see what God has done, how awesome his works on man's behalf." (Psalm 66:5)

PHOTO © School of Human Flight, Quincy, FL

SKY DIVING

A plane circled over the stadium. The crowd pointed skyward as people, looking like tiny dots, spewed from the back of the plane. One by one, the highly-skilled paratroopers descended, landing precisely on the circle marking centerfield. Ground spotters assisted, grabbing the chutes and making sure the jumpers landed softly. It doesn't always go that smoothly. We once saw a group of skilled paratroopers dressed as Elvis perform at a football game. A sudden gust of wind cause one of the "Flying Elvi" to collide with the goalpost. He hung helplessly, suspended by the cords of his chute, resulting in a dramatic rescue.

When my husband was in the army, he attended Airborne School. During their jumps, his class had some harrowing experiences with tangled chutes and rough landings. They had no assistance other than a crusty drill sergeant yelling orders with a bullhorn from below.

My sister's family went sky diving to celebrate their daughter's graduation, jumping in tandem. With a certified instructor, and with spotters waiting to assist when they reached the ground, their jumps went smoothly.

At times, when we face unexpected challenges, we must jump from the security of our "plane." Don't go it alone. Jump in tandem, held in the arms of our certified instructor, Jesus. And when we see others facing difficulties, we shouldn't be like the army drill sergeants, just barking criticism and advice from afar. We can come alongside, providing assistance and a soft place to land. Our help and prayers can ensure that they land on their feet.

"[He] comforts us in all our troubles so that we can comfort those in any trouble with the comfort we ourselves receive from God." (2 Corinthians 1:3-4)

PHOTO © Jana Osterlund

ROUND AND ROUND

The traveling carnival came to town. We watched with anticipation as the rides were constructed, the midway designed, and the concessions readied. There in the center—adorned with bright, gyrating lights—stood a majestic Ferris wheel. Driving down the highway, we could see it for miles, beckoning all who passed to come and enjoy. Round and round, up and down. A Ferris wheel provides fun, thrills and enjoyment; but it goes nowhere.

King Solomon, in his vast wisdom, saw life much like this. In the book of Ecclesiastes he writes that there is nothing new under the sun. He concludes that all is meaningless. We seek pleasure, we seek wealth, we work hard, but nothing is lasting. Round and round, up and down, but going nowhere, just like the Ferris wheel.

This is a pretty depressing and sobering view of life. Yet it is true that we spend much of our lives chasing after meaningless wealth, work, and pleasure that—when all is said and done—is like chasing after the wind. Meaningless.

Solomon concludes that 1) the ability to work, accomplish things, and enjoy life is a gift from God. We should revere him and be grateful for this gift, and 2) it is important to fear God and keep his commandments. This alone is of eternal value. We will someday be judged for what we've done, good or bad. When we follow God, we will indeed go somewhere—our eternal heavenly home, where we will have accumulated heavenly, lasting treasure. That is not meaningless.

"But store up for yourselves treasures in heaven, where moths and rust do not destroy and thieves do not break in and steal." (Matthew 6:20)

PHOTO © Susan Roberts

ROAD CONSTRUCTION DELAYS

Another delay. A lane is closed for repaving, and traffic is backed up for miles. It is especially frustrating when it appears that no one is working on the vast expanse of roadway that has been inhibited by cones. I must confess that I find these delays exasperating, especially when I am in a hurry. My patience runs thin. I get irritable. However, nothing I do will make traffic move any quicker. No effort on my part will get the project done sooner. So I wait. I have to remind myself that the finished product of smooth roads and extra lanes will be worth the trouble.

I get pretty impatient when God is doing one of his "construction projects" too. I really want to see the outcome and have things fixed right away. It is especially difficult when nothing seems to be happening. But God is working. He wants us to wait on him and rest in him for his best and perfect timing. He knows exactly what he is doing. David reminds us over and over in the Psalms to wait patiently with expectation. When we ask, we can be assured that the Lord will hear and answer. Don't fret. Take heart and be strong. Wait for his plan to unfold. God will answer! Trust that what he will accomplish will be a remarkable finished project.

"Morning by morning, O Lord, you hear my voice. Morning by morning, I lay my requests before you and wait in expectation." (Psalm 5:3)

PHOTO © CanStockPhoto Inc/ Noonie

WHAT THE HAWK DID

I looked out the window into our backyard and saw a huge, majestic hawk land on the arbor, right outside our kitchen window. It was so close that I could admire its colors and impressive stature. I praised God for this incredible part of his creation. I had never felt that way when a sparrow or starling landed on the arbor. This bird was something special. Then the hawk lifted its wings and pooped, placing a large dollop on our sidewalk. That rather destroyed the praise moment. I then realized that even this disgusting action is part of the "hawkness" that God created.

Not every aspect of creation seems pleasant and beautiful. Our humanness is not always admirable. We encounter people who make us uncomfortable, and can be disgusted by their actions, habits, appearance, and especially their sin. Other people may seem kind of nondescript—sort of like sparrows—and hardly worth our attention. We need to realize that all people, not just the lovely ones or special ones, are created in God's image, and loved by him. As Christians, we are called to accept and love people as they are, without showing favoritism, just as Jesus accepted us with all our imperfections. Let us pray to see people as God sees them, and love them as he loves them.

> "If you really keep the royal law found in Scripture, 'Love your neighbor as yourself,' you are doing right. But if you show favoritism, you sin and are convicted by the law as lawbreakers." (James 2:8-9)

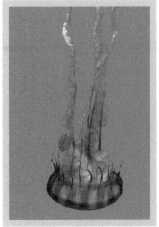

PHOTO © Susan Roberts

FROM BEAUTY TO BEAST

The pleasantness of a summer afternoon at the beach was suddenly shattered. I was floating lazily in the gentle ocean surf off West Palm Beach, Florida, when I felt a sharp sting. Then another and another. I screamed and my husband swam over to assist. I had become entangled in the tentacles of a jellyfish, and each movement caused more stings and welts. My husband brushed the silver threads away, being stung himself, but I was finally free. He helped me swim to the shore where a lifeguard assisted with a solution of baking soda and ammonia to ease the pain. Days later, though the pain had subsided, I was still covered with residual welts, looking much like I had been beaten with a stick.

Jellyfish are beautiful, ethereal creatures that are fascinating to watch. I spent hours at the Monterey Bay Aquarium watching them slowly rise and fall as if to a mesmerizing dance. It was hard to imagine they could be so dangerous.

Satan is like that. The Bible tells us that he masquerades as an angel of light, luring the unsuspecting into his dangerous traps (*see* 2 Corinthians 10:14). His temptations may appear harmless. We may be able to rationalize them away. They may even seem attractive. He is the great deceiver, the father of lies, and will appeal to all our senses to draw us from God's truth.

"So put on all of God's armor. Evil days will come. But you will be able to stand up to anything." (Ephesians 6:13, NIrV)

PHOTO © Susan Roberts

CONTRAIL

We watched a speck of a jet streak across the sky leaving a long stringed contrail. Soon both the jet and its mark in the sky were gone—vapor in the wind, quickly fading. The Bible tells us we are like that—grass withering and dying, flowers quickly fading, vapor in the wind (*see* James 4:14, Psalm 103:14-16). Sometimes jet contrails linger and spread wider, and sometimes they are instantly gone.

I believe our time here is also set—numbered by our almighty Creator (*see* Psalm 39:4-6; Job 14:5). I looked for scripture about making a mark or impression on earth while we are here. I didn't find any. It really isn't about us. Like Solomon says, "It's all vanity!" Yet we seek to be remembered and have significance while we are here. Few of us get statues or monuments, and even those are destroyed and forgotten. Yet how much time we spend trying to establishing our "mark": whether it is a financial legacy through a business or an inheritance, accolades and respect, or friendships and family. Leaving a mark on earth is not as important as we may think. Matthew 6:19-21 reminds us to make our mark in heaven, one that is eternal and will not fade.

"If any man builds on this foundation using gold, silver, costly stones, wood, hay or straw, his work will be shown for what it is, because the Day will bring it to light. It will be revealed with fire, and the fire will test the quality of each man's work. If what he has built survives, he will receive his reward."
(1 Corinthians 3:12-14)

PHOTO © Susan Roberts

GATOR BOYS

My daughter and son-in-law like to watch the TV series on Animal Planet called "Gator Boys." A call comes in to the headquarters from some family or business that needs to be rescued from the threat of an alligator. A couple of burly, fearless young men retrieve nuisance gators from golf courses, parking lots, backyard pools and garages. Sometimes a wayward gator even enters a house through a doggie door and ends up in a kitchen or bedroom. The men snag the alligators with a noose, and wrestle them until they can duct tape their mouths shut. The gators are then humanely released into the wild, away from human habitation. The homeowners are most relieved and grateful.

Almost every day when I drive to work, I see a "close call" where an inattentive driver is almost in an accident. To be honest, I have had a few of those myself. I find myself thanking and praising God for his protection. I think my guardian angels are frequently removing "gators" from out of my way. What a relief! I make an effort to remember to call on God for his protection before I leave the house, whether it is a short stint or a long haul. He will answer and come to my aid. How grateful I am to be rescued from these lurking dangers!

"For he will command his angels concerning you, to guard you in all your ways; 'Because he loves me,' says the Lord, 'I will rescue him; I will protect him, for he acknowledges my name.'" (Psalm 91:11,14)

PHOTO © Marilyn Osborne

HAIL

A boom of thunder. A flash of lightning. Pelting rain. Looking out the window, to the west we see blue sky. Some parts of our town got hail—lots of it! People even had to get out and shovel what looked like snow—in July. Yet a mile away streets are dry. I guess this is what you call scattered storms. Crazy Colorado.

We have had a front-row seat to this demonstration of our Creator's power. We think there is no better entertainment. David declared, "He spreads the snow like wool and scatters the frost like ashes. He hurls down his hail like pebbles. Who can withstand his icy blast? He sends his word and melts them; lightning and hail, snow and clouds, that do his bidding, let them praise the name of the Lord, for his name alone is exalted; his splendor is above the earth and the heavens" (Psalm 147:16-18, 148:8).

I guess I like storms because they are a wonderful reminder of our great, awesome God whom even the waves and winds obey. I like to watch his might and creativity at work. This same God, who can control the weather, also walks beside us to manage our own inner storms. If he is able to orchestrate the weather with his power and might, surely he is able to help those who put their trust in him.

"For I am the Lord, your God, who takes hold of your right hand, and says to you, 'Do not fear; I will help you.'" (Isaiah 41:13)

PHOTO © Dr. Ed Holroyd

UNSTUCK

We had some excitement at our house while our daughter and her family were visiting recently. Our young grandson came running up from the basement screaming. His family had been playing soccer downstairs and discovered that a prairie dog had fallen into the window well. We tried to remove him, but the more we tugged, the more he buried himself in the dirt with only his butt and tail showing. I finally got a garden trowel and dug through the hard dirt to unearth enough of him so we could grab him and pull him out. He was not happy. I'm sure he was very scared with all the commotion, yelling and yanking. We had to do it for his own good or he would've died. We released him into the backyard, and hopefully he found his way back to his colony. Perhaps he learned his lesson and will stay away from houses in the future.

Like the prairie dog, we get ourselves into fixes and find we are stuck in an unhealthy relationship, lifestyle, or occupation. Though we might not realize it at the time, we desperately need God to come to our rescue. Sometimes he disciplines us by altering our course pretty abruptly, with us unhappily resisting. We become full of anxiety and fear. Though this is unpleasant, we must eventually learn that everything God does is for our good because he loves us. He wants us to be free and to prosper.

Accepting God's discipline with humility, and learning from it, leads to a fulfilled life.

> "No discipline seems pleasant at the time, but painful. Later on, however, it produces a harvest of righteousness and peace for those who have been trained by it." (Hebrews 12:11)

PHOTO © Susan Roberts

THE MIGHTY TONGUE

We all have something pretty remarkable hiding in the inside of our mouths. These little organs, each consisting of eight muscles, and measuring about ten centimeters, are our tongues. They have a variety of important functions including tasting, crushing and digesting food, swallowing, cleaning teeth and assisting speech. The tongue is covered with tiny taste buds that help us distinguish between bitter, sweet, salty, sour, and spicy foods, making our meals more enjoyable.

However, this organ can be a troublemaker. For such a little guy, it can pack a tremendous punch. In the Bible, James calls it "a restless evil full of deadly poison that no one can tame. It corrupts the whole person and sets the whole course of his life on fire by hell"… anyone who considers himself religious, and yet does not keep a tight rein on his tongue, deceives himself and his religion is worthless" (James 1:26, 3:6-9). This seemingly insignificant muscle can both worship God and curse men.

Solomon also has some pretty harsh words to say about the tongue. He rails against lying, deceitful, flattering tongues that give a false witness, slander neighbors, and speak folly. Yet, the tongue can be used for good purposes. Solomon also notes that a guarded tongue is wise and valuable like silver. Pleasant words are soothing and healing, bringing joy and peace. As we go through our day today, let us rely on the power of the Holy Spirit to do the taming of the tongue. Let us use this incredible little organ for good, not evil.

"The tongue has the power of life and death." (Proverbs 18:21)

PHOTO © Susan Roberts

BRAND NAMES

I'm sure you've noticed that the brand names of things are often indicative of the ownership or the characteristics of the product. For instance, brands like Hershey®, Kellogg®, and Ford® link the product to the owner/founder. Other names like Minute Tapioca®, Chunky Soup®, Nice and Easy®, and Tuff Shed® give a pretty good idea of what the product is like or the intended result (although they do not always deliver as promised).

Early Christ followers were first called Christians in Antioch (see Acts 11:26). When we call ourselves "Christian," we are taking on the name that indicates both the founder and his characteristics. As follows of Christ we endeavor to be like him—a true representative who brings honor to his name and lives up to the standard. Paul told the early Christians at Thessalonica that "We constantly pray for you, that our God may make you worthy of his calling, and that by his power he may fulfill every good purpose of yours and every act prompted by your faith. We pray this so that the name of our Lord Jesus may be glorified in you, and you in him, according to the grace of our God and the Lord Jesus Christ" (2 Thessalonians 1:11-12). Let us also pray for each other that we may live up to the label of Christian, glorifying Jesus in all we do.

"And whatever you do, whether in word or deed, do it all in the name of the Lord Jesus, giving thanks to God the Father through him." (Colossians 3:17)

PHOTO © Susan Roberts

CEILING FANS

On warm nights our bedroom feels stuffy. When stagnant air makes sleep difficult, I enjoy turning on the ceiling fan for a refreshing breeze, which helps me rest. We'd like to put ceiling fans in our new home, too, so we've been shopping for deals online. We found a website with hundreds of styles, shapes, colors, sizes and prices. Who knew there was so much out there. We found big fans with lots of little fans attached to the blades. There were strange-looking rods with multiple box fans hanging in assorted directions. We had to laugh when we saw vintage airplane fans, where the propeller was the ceiling fan. To each his own. Whatever the style, I am sure they accomplish what ceiling fans are meant to do.

Sometimes my spirit feels stuffy and stagnant too. I don't feel like I am moving forward. I'm not sure where to go next. I have trouble resting in the Lord and waiting on him. Then the refreshing breath of God's Spirit wafts over me. his love assures me I can trust him. I rest in the peace beyond understanding.

Each of us has access to the refreshing love and peace that God's Spirit gives. God meets our unique needs in a personal way. He knows each of us intimately and is there to breathe life and hope into our weary spirits, so that we might find rest in him.

"The Lord is my shepherd...He refreshes my soul." (Psalm 23:1-3)

PHOTO © Susan Roberts

YORKSHIRE PUDDING

You've probably heard of tea and crumpets, but what are some other British foods? Well, there's *bangers and mash, bubbles and squeak*, and *Yorkshire pudding*. Our granddaughter had a school project about England, and she needed to come up with a food for her class to sample. We decided on Yorkshire pudding. I researched recipes and found a distinctly British one online. It was a challenge converting the grams of flour, milliliters of milk and Celsius temperature to American measurements. We followed the recipe and were quite pleased with the results. The batter is poured into hot oil and it puffs up while cooking. When it cools, a hole forms in the middle, and it sinks. The British serve this as a side with pot roast, filling the well in the "pudding" with mashed potatoes and/or mushroom gravy.

As we watched the pastries puff in the hot oven, I thought about how we, too, can think we're "hot stuff" and get all puffed up with pride. When we are "full of ourselves" God cannot use us. The Bible tells us that pride goes before a fall (*see* Proverbs 16:18). However, when we humble ourselves before the Lord, and deflate our pride, he can fill us with good things and make us much more usable for his purposes. When we humble ourselves before him, he will lift us up (*see* James 4:10).

"God opposes the proud but gives grace to the humble." (1 Peter 5:5b)

PHOTO © Chris Roberts

PHOTO © Susan Roberts

PHOTO © Jana Osterlund

WHAT'S YOUR PREFERENCE?

What is the best way to cook a steak? I watched Iron Chef Bobby Flay's tutorial. He gave advice on seasoning, searing, and grilling that is supposed to be the definitive answer. However, I discovered there are many ways to grill a steak. People have secret marinades and wet and dry rubs. Opinions vary on using gas grills, charcoal or even pan searing. And, of course, preferences differ concerning doneness. I like mine medium rare.

Unfortunately, people approach God in much the same way. Opinions differ regarding who he is and how he works. To some, he is a big meanie. To others he is a namby-pamby God, unable to do much. Perhaps he is silent and uninvolved, setting the world in motion, but not really caring what happens until the end. Is he a genie that we come to when we have a wish? Maybe he is not really there; he exists only in the imagination of the weak and needy. One might say that everyone is entitled to their own opinion, but while this might work for cooking steaks, it doesn't work for knowing God. We cannot turn him into a God of our own choosing. But we can know him—Jesus made sure of that when his sacrifice reconciled us to God. Now, as God's children, we are in a lifelong pursuit of getting to know who he really is.

> "My purpose is that they may be encouraged in heart and united in love so that they may have the full riches of complete understanding, in order that they may know the mystery of God, namely Christ, in whom are hidden all the treasures of wisdom and knowledge." (Colossians 2:2-3)

PHOTO © Susan Roberts

LET'S EAT!

Our young grandson was saying grace, thanking God for everyone and everything that came to his mind—dogs, cats, the zoo, pretty flowers, sunshine, the playground, the car, his house—all of this, plus all his friends, family and teachers. Oblivious to the food getting cold, he went on and on until an adult stopped him. (Enough already. Let's eat!)

Historically, the head of the family says grace, but many families take turns. Those with young children may recite a scripted prayer like "God is great, God is good, let us thank him for our food." It is a wonderful tradition to take a moment to acknowledge God's goodness before meals, thanking him for his gifts to us. This should be something we do earnestly—not just a hurried habit.

Our grandson may have been closer to the real idea of grace. It is important that we take the time to thank God for all the things he has done for us. Grace is God's undeserved favor, and we all are benefactors of his awesome generosity. Each day, each possession, each person in our lives and all creation around us are gifts to us from God. Grace should not be just a simple, quick prayer that we say before a meal, but a way of life—noticing throughout the day what God has done and is doing, and offering him our heartfelt praise.

"Give thanks to the Lord, call on his name; make known among the nations what he has done. Sing to him, sing praise to him, tell of all his wonderful acts." (1 Chronicles 16: 8-9)

PHOTO © Perry Roberts

CAN YOU HEAR ME NOW?

The phone rings, the doorbell dings, the cell phone beeps, the dog barks, the kids are tussling, deadlines loom. Places to go. Things to do. Does this sound familiar? In the hustle and bustle of life, quiet can be an elusive thing. It is defined as freedom from noise, but also can be freedom from turmoil, anxiety, impatience and pride. People have trouble with quiet when it is freedom from activity. The absence of something to do can be unnerving. Silence makes people agitated. Have you ever been in a group discussion when there was a lengthy silence? Soon everyone is casting sideways glances and fidgeting. But comfort with quiet is a healthy quality to develop.

Psalm 46 is a "noisy" Psalm with mountains crashing, seas roaring, and nations warring. So it almost seems incongruous that verse 10 tells us to "Be still and know that I am God." How in the world can we be still and listen in the midst of all that roaring and static and distraction? Our minds can be too busy to have a very clear channel. Yet, the Psalm also tells us that God is our strength and fortress (vs. 1). We can escape the hectic noise of life by running to him for peace and quiet, refreshment and renewal. Quiet is also defined as being well-tuned (as in an engine), which requires regular maintenance. Satan works hard to destroy our quiet time—prayer and Bible reading—with disruptions, but we can pray that God shelters us from the noise and gives us a clear channel to hear him.

"Be still and know that I am God." (Psalm 46:10)

PHOTO © Susan Roberts

LET'S SEE WHAT DEVELOPS

Do you remember the days before digital cameras? Pictures were taken, and there was often a wait of up to a week to receive prints back. It sure has been convenient snapping pictures of our grandkids with our cell phones, and then sending instantly to others with just a push of a button. In college, my husband took a photography class, taking photos with black and white 35mm film. He learned to go into the dark room, close the door, turn off the lights, and immerse the negatives in the developing solution to literally see what developed. The negatives from the camera showed the picture in reverse—so it was hard to make out the image prior to the process. Everything was unclear in the beginning, but the end result brought clarity.

How interesting that the unprocessed film is called "negatives." Many times, as we are becoming what God wants us to be, there are "negatives." Circumstances cause things to be dark and unclear. We sometimes forget that we are in the midst of the process. We focus on the present with all its cloudiness and reverses. If we immerse ourselves in God instead, his Spirit will change us into a clear image of himself. "Until God opens the next door, praise him in the hallway."[9] We can thank and praise God even before we see his solution, trusting that he indeed is developing a plan.

"For I know the plans I have for you,' declares the Lord, 'plans to prosper you and not to harm you, plans to give you hope and a future.'" (Jeremiah 29:11)

9. Title of an article by Kelly Wahlquist in *CatholicMom.com*, April 22, 2013

PHOTO © Susan Roberts

PUZZLES

My husband's sisters love to do puzzles. The more pieces and pattern details, the more pleasure they derive from the challenge. It is fun to watch the picture take shape, though the messy process may hold the dining-room table hostage for a long time. Eventually the picture is revealed as all the pieces are fitted.

When our kids were little, we read from a book, *Purple Puzzle Tree*. The overall theme was that God, throughout history, gradually acts, and adds "pieces" of truth to reveal his plan for us and the world. From the moment sin entered the world through Adam and Eve, God began a plan of salvation. It was mirrored in the laws and sacrifices of the Israelites. More pieces were added by the prophets, as they foretold of the coming Messiah. When Jesus came, he was the fulfilment of the first part of God's plan—a Savior who would conquer death and take away the sins of the world (*see* Romans 16:25-26). Someday we will see the completion of God's plan as Jesus comes again and establishes a New Heaven and New Earth.

"And he made known to us the mystery of his will according to his good pleasure, which he purposed in Christ, to be put into effect when the times will have reached their fulfillment—to bring all things in heaven and on earth together under one head, even Christ." (Ephesians 1:9-10)

PHOTO © Bill Cassell

FIRST RESPONDERS

They donned their gear and stormed the building. Our son-in-law's brother was conducting an exercise with the SWAT team in Las Vegas. He has told us how they practice their methods of "First Response" to various crisis scenarios. The procedures become so ingrained with the team that they can act automatically, almost without thinking. They know exactly what to do and how to do it.

We face a lot of "crises" in our lives. What is your "first response?" Do you cuss or yell? Do you panic or worry? Or, do you pray and praise? When we stay close to Jesus by praying, reading God's Word, and dwelling on his truths, we store up the confidence and calm we will need for unexpected difficulties. His power changes our spirits and gives us the presence of mind and strength to tackle the problems automatically with grace. Our first response can then be one of peace instead of anger or panic.

We visited my Mom in Florida who was suffering from Alzheimer's disease. Although she was often confused and agitated, she constantly sang hymns to herself, forgetting the words, but knowing that she could find God's strength in her music. In spite of her illness and inability to orchestrate her reactions, her first response, from a lifetime with Jesus, was a peaceful spirit.

> "Finally, brothers, whatever is true, whatever is noble, whatever is right, whatever is pure, whatever is lovely, whatever is admirable—if anything is excellent or praiseworthy—think about such things. Whatever you have learned or received or heard from me, or seen in me—put it into practice. And the God of peace will be with you." (Philippians 4:8-9)

PHOTO © Brooke Roberts

SWIMMING

I remember being very afraid of water as a young child. A camp swimming instructor actually threw me in the deep end of a pool. I don't recommend this technique; but it did literally teach me to sink or swim, as the instructor cheered me on and congratulated me on my success. From then on, I was confident in the water and I eventually even became a life guard and swimming instructor.

Our young granddaughter was also not thrilled about the water. It took her a while to become comfortable and enjoy it. As her confidence and daring increased, my daughter-in-law had to remain very vigilant to protect her from the trouble that could come as a result of her independence and exuberance.

There are lots of things that come up in our lives that make us reluctant to "get our feet wet": perhaps a move or a new job; maybe a medical issue requiring scary surgery or treatments; or a call to a new ministry. We don't always have the option of easing in, but find ourselves dumped into situations with no preparation. We flounder and try to catch our breath. In spite of unpleasantness and fear, we can have confidence that God will not leave us. Eventually, we will discover that God has good in store for us and we can take the plunge. He cheers us on, ever vigilant to protect us from harm. As we gain confidence, though, we do need to stay close to him and not get carried away by our independence and exuberance.

"When I am afraid, I will trust in you....Therefore my heart is glad and my tongue rejoices; my body also will rest secure, because you will not abandon me."
(Psalm 56:3, 16:9-10)

PHOTO © Carol Cassell

IN HIS IMAGE

The relatives gathered and *oohed* and *aahed* at the new arrival. "She looks like her mom, but she has her dad's nose," an aunt observed. "With those long fingers, she'll surely play piano like me," her grandmother concluded.

We are created in the image of God. What does that mean? God doesn't have a physical form that we can "look" like. We certainly do not have his majesty, power, and wisdom. He is so much bigger than we are, it is hard to compare us to him at all. Yet, the Bible says we are created in his image.

As I write this, I am designing a new house. I am keenly aware that my ability to create is a little piece of God in me. Anthony Hoekema wrote: "Anytime someone invents a machine, writes a book, paints a landscape, enjoys a symphony, calculates a sum, or names a pet, he or she is proclaiming the fact that we are made in God's image."[10] We also reflect God's image in our ability to think and reason. We are social beings, able to feel emotions like love, pleasure, and sadness, just like our Father. We can communicate with each other. God has instilled in us a moral conscience, an ability to choose, and an awareness of him. Our very essence is in God's image, and one day, as we are resurrected, we will even more fully reflect his likeness.

As members of God's family, let us work to be ever more conformed to his image and the image of his Son, so that others will see him in us.

"For those God foreknew he also predestined to be conformed to the likeness of his Son, among many brothers." (Romans 8:29)

10. Anthony Hoekema, *Created In God's Image* (Eerdmans, 1994).

PHOTO © Carol Cassell

LOOK IN THE MIRROR

Who can make the funniest face? The silly images we saw caused ripples of giggles. Though it's fun, clowning is not the normal use of a mirror. Rather, a mirror helps us make sure everything is in order. Before going anywhere, we want to check for spinach in teeth, tags sticking out, smudges on faces, or wayward cowlicks. What we see may indeed be motivation for change. We may just need a minor adjustment. It might be time for a new look, a makeover, exercise or weight loss. Mirrors do help us be aware of how we present ourselves. Can you imagine what it would be like to go several days, a month, or even a year without checking the mirror? We'd become pretty scruffy and unkempt.

We certainly pay attention to our physical appearance, but spiritual wellbeing is even more important. We should make frequent checks to ensure all is in order. That might mean committing to a prayer time, a Bible-reading plan, a small group. Real change to physical appearance doesn't happen overnight. Neither does a spiritual change. Sedentary people start with small steps. Walkers try jogging. 5Kers try half marathons. It is the same with our spiritual development—we start with little steps so we are not discouraged, and gradually work up to greater things. Eventually, with God's help, we will begin to see the reflection we want—a reflection of Jesus. Look in God's mirror, and see what adjustments you need to make. Then, with God's help, improve your reflection.

"And we, who with unveiled faces all reflect the Lord's glory, are being transformed into his likeness with ever-increasing glory, which comes from the Lord, who is the Spirit." (2 Corinthians 3:18)

PHOTO © Susan Roberts

FITBIT

How many steps did you take? How many flights of stairs did you climb? This has been a topic of conversation when our kids get together. Our kids and grandkids have Fitbits, and there is some good-natured competition to see who accomplishes the most. The days' target is 10,000 steps, and they are rewarded with a green light when they get there. The bottom line is that this motivates them to work at staying in shape. They had to learn all the ins and outs of using their devices—tracking their progress, syncing them to their phones and even sharing their milestones with others. Of course there are ways to cheat. Sometimes just moving arms or bouncing can affect the tally. That rather defeats the purpose, though.

Physical training does take commitment, motivation and effort. So does spiritual training. Neither will be very productive if corners are cut. David encourages us to run in the paths of God's commands, and not run in our own way. "Keep me from deceitful ways; be gracious to me and teach me your law. I have chosen the way of faithfulness; I have set my heart on your laws. I hold fast to your statutes, Lord, do not let me be put to shame. I run in the path of your commands, for you have broadened my understanding" (Psalm 119:29-32, NIVUK). As we do our spiritual training, God is there behind us cheering us on too. Listen to his voice and be encouraged in your daily walk.

"Whether you turn to the right or to the left, your ears will hear a voice behind you, saying, 'This is the way; walk in it.'" (Isaiah 30:21)

PHOTO © Joyce Kepto

I'VE GOT TO HAVE A PONY

When I was little, I wanted a pony. I begged and begged. It was a very impractical request given the residential neighborhood in which I lived. The desire was somewhat pacified by numerous pony rides, trail rides and eventually week-long stays at a Christian dude ranch in New Hampshire.

When I was in college, I spent summers working at a Christian Camp in upstate New York. When the directors learned of my love for horses, they brought in two for the campers to ride, and gave me the responsibility of caring for them. At first it was fun. I could ride them whenever I wished, and race bareback across the meadow. They were rather unruly, and if they got out of the pasture, it often took me several hours to catch them. They relieved themselves on the director's front steps. They ate flower beds. After a while, the hard work and responsibility took its toll and I decided I really didn't want to own a horse after all.

We ask God over and over again to do something and get frustrated when we can't get what we want. God understands, better than we do, what is practical and best for us. We cannot see the whole picture. God might even give us what we ask for, and then we find it is not what we wanted after all. We ask him for the desires of our hearts, but our desires might not be aligned to his. Sometimes his timing makes us wait. But we can be fully confident that he does have our best interest at heart. Trust him. Wait patiently for him.

> "Delight yourselves in the Lord and he will give you the desires of your heart."
> (Psalm 37:4)

PHOTO © Susan Roberts

NO LANTERN

My parents came to visit us when we lived in Washington State. We were eager to show them around, so we took them to see the Pacific Ocean. We walked down a steep evergreen-lined path to the beach, played in the surf, and walked on the sand. We were treated to a gorgeous sunset.

No one wanted to leave, so we found some driftwood and a lighter and built a fire on the beach. We laughed, talked and sang until it was very dark.

There was no moon. As we headed back to the car, we realized that once we were in the trees, the darkness totally obscured the path. We couldn't see our hands in front of our faces. We held onto each other and gingerly made our way up the hill, but we bumped into trees, and nearly slipped down some embankments. My Dad walked into a tree and ended up with a nasty shiner.

We really wished for a flashlight! Much to our relief, we did eventually make it back with only minor bumps and scratches.

Without a light we slip and slide, stumble and fall. We can get misdirected or hurt. Others can help, but they really are not sufficient. In the walk of life, we need to rely on the light of God's Word to show us the path, help us avoid pitfalls, and get us safely home.

"Your word is a lamp to my feet and a light for my path." (Psalm 119:105)

PHOTO © Brooke Roberts

AT THE HEART

Our family loves artichokes. We buy them when we find them on sale and have experimented with growing them in our garden. Part of the attraction is the fun of eating them. We peel off the bitter outer petals, then dip the others in butter, scrape off the good stuff with our teeth, then toss the remains into a bowl in the center of the table. The tossing becomes a game with whooping and hollering if someone makes the shot, and groans when they miss. People have a hard time believing that our little grandkids like artichokes. They seem like something for a more mature palate. My husband has often commented that he wonders who came up with the idea of eating artichokes in the first place—they certainly do not appear appetizing with their spiny, fibrous involucre bracts. The real treat is the delectable heart in the center, but it takes quite a bit of effort to get there.

Many times in life we have "dishes" placed before us that do not appear appetizing. What we are served in life may be bitter, spiny and fibrous. It seems like a lot of work to find a tiny bit of joy in all that trouble. We can be assured, however, that God has our best interest in mind. At the heart of the challenge is a blessing, if we will take the time and make the effort, with God's help, to get there.

> "Taste and see that the Lord is good; blessed is the man who takes refuge in him. Fear the Lord, you his saints, for those who fear him lack nothing. The lions may grow weak and hungry, but those who seek the Lord lack no good thing."
> (Psalm 34:8-10)

PHOTO © Susan Roberts

PICKING VEGGIES

Harvest is a rewarding time when we can literally see the fruits of our hard work. Last spring we had cleaned away the debris, prepared the soil, removed the weeds, sowed the seeds, watered and fertilized—all preparing for this moment. We were excited when the first vegetables were ready to pick. Whoops. We forgot our basket for carrying vegetables. Oh well, our T-shirts will work just fine. We collected a variety of produce and headed to the kitchen, where we prepared some of the veggies for our dinner. Not only do the fresh veggies taste great, but this culmination of our labors makes them especially wonderful.

Jesus talks about a different kind of harvest—that of bringing people into God's kingdom. He said, "Open your eyes and look at the fields. They are ripe for harvest" (John 4:35). People need the Lord and we have been given the directive to tell them about him. We have been called to go into the fields yet we all have different functions. Some of us clean up sinful influences and endeavor to prepare people to be receptive to God. Others plant seeds of truth that are watered by the efforts of others. The harvesters can then come along and bring people to Jesus. It might be in a conventional way of preaching or teaching; or it might be an unconventional method of life-style evangelism. Each of us should perform our God-given task.

> "We each carried out our servant assignment. I planted the seed, Apollos watered the plants, but God made you grow. It's not the one who plants or the one who waters who is at the center of this process but God, who makes things grow."
> (1 Corinthians 3:6-7, The Message)

PHOTO © Susan Roberts

MONSTER ZUCCHINI

Fresh vegetables sounded like a great addition to our dinner, so I headed down to my garden to see what was ripe. I picked some lettuce, tomatoes, cucumbers and herbs for a salad, and some green beans to steam. When I moved a zucchini leaf, I was amazed to see a monster squash the size of a baseball bat, lying there in the dirt. Where had that come from? I had picked zucchinis several times over the past few days, but this giant had eluded me, well hidden in the leaves. What was I going to do with this huge vegetable? Thankfully, my sister-in-law shared a "zucchini boat" recipe that fit the bill.

When Adam and Eve sinned, they covered themselves with leaves and hid from God, but God wasn't fooled. God came looking for them, and though they had to be punished by leaving the garden, he continued to love them and pursue a relationship with them. When we have sinned, we too, like Adam, want to hide from God. Our transgressions make us feel alienated from him. Psalm 139:7-10 tells us that God is everywhere and knows everything about us. Nothing is hidden from him. Instead of hiding *from* God when we have sinned, we need to hide *in* God. He loves us, and nothing can separate us from that love—not even our sin, he wants to forgive us, comfort us, shelter us and help us.

"For in the day of trouble he will keep me safe in his dwelling; he will hide me in the shelter of his tabernacle..."
(Psalm 27:5)

PHOTO © Brooke Roberts

WHAT'S COOKING?

Labor Day is considered the last hurrah of summer. After the long weekend, we get back into the routine of work, school, church programs and schedules. Vacations are over.

For Labor Day celebrations with family and friends, many Americans cook out on a grill, with meat as the main event. (Except for vegetarians) Many cooks go to great lengths, often using secret recipes, to produce the best entrée. Surprisingly, though, Labor Day comes in third as the "grilliest holiday"—preceded by Memorial Day and the Fourth of July. In fact, polls show that 74% of Americans cook outside. Beef products top the wanted list (steaks, burgers), followed by hotdogs and chicken.[11]

Hebrews 5:13-14 exhorts us to grow up from using "baby's milk" to eating the "meat" in God's Word—so that our spiritual senses become sharp and we can discern good from evil. Imagine going to a Labor Day celebration where the host served baby food! How disappointing and unappetizing. Yet, when it comes to God's Word, we are more comfortable with simple and familiar spiritual food. We'd rather be fed easy formulas than pick up utensils to feed ourselves. It takes work to find the food and chew on the more difficult doctrines and principles. Yet that's how we grow up Christ.

"Grow in the grace and knowledge of our Lord and Savior Jesus Christ."
(2 Peter 3:18)

11. Statistics published in *The Business Journal PR Newswire* (May 25, 2016), and *HPBA: Fun Facts About Barbeque* www.hpba.org/consumers/barbeque/fun-facts-about-barbeque)

PHOTO © Susan Roberts

WHERE IS OUR TRUST?

"I pledge allegiance to the flag..." Most of us have recited this many times.
It isn't as popular now, though. Political correctness deems the Pledge of
Allegiance inappropriate and offensive. However, many of us are still proud
to place our hands on our hearts and honor this country and its flag. Our
Pledge is unique because it does not affirm a particular political party or
policy. It unites us as citizens of a great nation.

The Pledge of Allegiance was written in 1892 by Francis Bellamy, a
Baptist minister. He had noticed that national pride was waning. He led
a highly successful campaign to place a flag in every American classroom
and have children recite the pledge each day. It was Mr. Bellamy's wish to
"instill into the minds of our American youth a love for their country and
the principles on which it was founded."

In 1942, the pledge was officially adopted by Congress, with the words
"Under God" added in 1954. George MacPherson Docherty, a Presbyterian
minister, encouraged this addition, when he said, "'Under God' is the defin-
ing phrase that sets the United States apart from other nations. Our nation's
might lays not in arms, but in its spirit and higher purpose."[1] President
Eisenhower heartily agreed. "Millions will daily proclaim the dedication of
our nation and our people to the Almighty, reaffirming the transcendence
of religious faith in America's heritage and future. In this way we shall
constantly strengthen those spiritual weapons which forever will be our

(Continued on next page)

country's most powerful resource, in peace or in war."[2] This is our heritage.

As our country moves into the future, we must remember that our strength and success does not result from our own efforts and ingenuity. Let us turn to our God, our source and strength, putting our trust in him alone.

> "Do not put your trust in princes, in mortal men who cannot save...Blessed is he whose help is the God of Jacob, whose hope is in the Lord his God."
> (Psalm 146:3-5)

---

12. From a sermon on February 2, 1954 at New York Ave. Presbyterian Church, titled "New Birth of Freedom."

13. Quoted in a PBS production titled "God In America: God In the White House," http://www.pbs.org/godinamerica/god-in-the-white-house.

PHOTO © Susan Roberts

NATIONAL DOUGHNUT DAY

Let's celebrate! June 2 is National Doughnut Day, and several places offer free doughnuts! Indulge your sweet tooth.

Doughnuts, according to one legend, were first invented by Elizabeth Gregory, the mother of a New England sea captain. She made the confections for the crew with ingredients from her son's spice-trading ship, and added nuts to the center for nutrition for the sailors—just like a mother! One story claims that her son, Hanson Gregory, was guiding the ship through a particularly fierce storm off the coast of Massachusetts. He needed to keep both hands on the wheel, so he jammed his doughnut onto a spoke, creating the first doughnut hole.[14] Regardless of the origins, doughnuts are a popular breakfast pastry, with more than two billion dollars in sales annually! Those of us with a sweet tooth particularly appreciate and even crave these tasty treats, breakfast or not.

We have a "sweet tooth" in our spirits too. We desire kind words which Proverbs calls "sweet to the soul and healing to the bones" (Proverbs 16:24). Other sweets for our spirit are God's promises and ordinances. Wisdom is another sweet that we can crave. It provides hope and a future (*see* Proverbs 24:14). These sweets are not empty calories like doughnuts. They are truly beneficial. Enjoy a doughnut on National Doughnut Day, but also crave, enjoy and share the sweets from God's Word.

His words "are sweeter than honey... in keeping them there is great reward."
(Psalm 19:10-11)

14. www.smithsonianmag.com/history/the-history-of-the-doughnut

PHOTO © Jana Osterlund

FATHERS

Fathers come in all different shapes and sizes. They take on many different roles. My dad was provider, driver, sports buddy, playmate, gardener, fix-it man, teacher, church leader and sounding board. He faithfully went to work each day, driving me to school on the way. When I struggled with math, he was my patient tutor; when I wrote something, he was my proofreader; when I learned to water ski, he drove the boat; and when I learned to drive, he was my stoic instructor. Anytime we played a game, he was there competing—SPUD, shuffleboard, "Oh Shucks," and checkers. I enjoyed yanking his chain by bringing up controversial issues. He offered sound financial advice and commented on gardening techniques. If the church doors were open, we piled in the car to attend services, youth groups and special events.

Not all dads are this involved, so I feel blessed to have a dad that cared. Even if you did not have a dad who was present, you do have a heavenly Father who cares even more than earthly dads. He listens to us and provides for us. He helps us and guides us. We don't have to withdraw in fear and stand in the shadows. God reaches for us with open arms and welcomes us into his presence where we can crawl up on his lap and talk to him like a daddy—"Abba, Father" (*see* Romans 8:15).

As we celebrate our earthly dads on Father's Day, let us also celebrate the loving, caring relationship we have with our heavenly Dad. He is all we need.

"Let us then approach the throne of grace with confidence, so that we may receive mercy and find grace to help us in our time of need." (Hebrews 4:16)

PHOTO © Susan Roberts

INDEPENDENCE DAY

On the fourth of July, we celebrate Independence Day. This is not when the Declaration of Independence was signed, but rather when the final draft was approved. The bulk of this document was written by Thomas Jefferson, who died on July 4, 1826—the fiftieth anniversary of the signing. This declaration was not intended to be a license for citizens to do as they pleased. It was envisioned to be a stepping stone away from tyrannical rule to a new and fair government that would allow life, liberty and the pursuit of happiness for all. It is interesting to note that the writers felt very strongly that the rights they wished to claim were "endowed by their Creator." Furthermore, in the declaration they expressed "a firm reliance on the protection of divine Providence."

As we celebrate our nation's Independence Day, let us also celebrate another kind of declaration of independence that is far more important. Romans 6:18 tells us we have been set free from sin. Just like our nation's founders, we are not free to do whatever we please. We leave the tyrannical rule of sin, and take on the life-giving leadership of God. We have become subject to God and his righteousness. Our life, liberty and pursuit of happiness is not dependent on our government's inception, but on our Savior's redemption.

> "Those who belong to Christ Jesus are no longer under God's judgment. Because of what Christ Jesus has done, you are free. You are now controlled by the law of the Holy Spirit who gives you life. The law of the Spirit frees you from the law of sin that brings death." (Romans 8:1-2, NIrV)

FALL

PHOTO © Susan Roberts

JUNK IS JUNK

As we drive around town, we see signs for garage sales, yards sales, estate sales and even barn sales. It seems like people are taking advantage of the last nice weekends of fall to clean house and get rid of junk. We smile as we remember a foreign visitor who asked about the meaning of the signs. "One person's junk is other person's treasure," she was told.

The visitor shook her head. "In my country, junk is junk!"

The Israelites had a way of taking on other nations' junk. It wasn't just their idols. They adopted their ways of doing business. They treated the less fortunate with contempt. The judged unfairly and were dishonest in transactions. They were self-centered and unkind. In all their ways, they forgot God and became self-sufficient and arrogant. This was hugely displeasing to God.

We may not take home idols, but we do buy into others' grumpy attitudes, gossip, worry, prejudices and indiscretions, and dishonest practices. We even treat people in our own families with disrespect. It seems that if someone else does it, it's OK for me to act in kind. But junk is junk and sin is sin. Our lives should not be about pleasing ourselves, but about pleasing God and laying up real eternal treasures in his kingdom.

"Don't become so well adjusted to your culture that you fit into it without even thinking. Instead, fix your attention on God. You'll be changed from the inside out. Readily recognize what he wants from you, and quickly respond to it. Unlike the culture around you, always dragging you down to its level of immaturity, God brings the best out of you, develops well-formed maturity in you."
(Romans 12:2, The Message)

PHOTO © Susan Roberts

NO QUICK FIX

I tripped over a luggage carrier and fell, severely injuring my shoulder. I had to have surgery and a follow-up of extensive physical therapy. I met with the therapist twice a week for eight months, following his advice and enduring the painful routine. I also had daily home exercises. It was hard to keep up with the regimen. It took several weeks just to be able to put a plastic cup on an eye-level shelf. How frustrating! I wished that there was a quick fix, like a pill or injection that would make my muscles strong and my tendons and joints work smoothly, without all this effort and inconvenience. But, there is no substitution for hard work and time.

We might treat our spiritual life in the same way. We wish there were a procedure like going to church, or an injection of a quick prayer or devotion that would strengthen us and allow us to perform life as an accomplished, successful Christian without all the extra effort. But, there is no substitute for multiple daily "work-outs" with God where we stretch our spiritual muscles, listen to his instruction, practice what he says and work to maintain our relationship of love with him and others. When we meet with God, he gives us the power to listen and move in accordance with his Spirit. When we neglect this, we stay weak and unresponsive.

"But those who wait upon the Lord shall renew their strength. They shall mount up with wings like eagles; they shall run and not be weary; they shall walk and not faint." (Isaiah 40:31, NKJV)

PHOTO © Jana Osterlund

THE HARBINGER

I love the colorful foliage of fall. We take drives in the mountains to see the changing leaves—neon yellow aspens set against the backdrop of deep green pines, punctuated by reds and oranges of various other trees and shrubs. The newscasters generally predict the best weekends to view the color, and as a result, mountain roadways are overcrowded with eager "leaf peepers."

Besides changing leaves, there are other signs of fall. One morning, we got up to find a layer of frost on our car windshield. We looked out at the mountain peaks that overnight had become bright white with fresh snow. The crispness in the air and shortened days let us know that fall was here.

Jesus tells us to pay attention to the signs of the times as we await his coming. We watch the perversion of truth, the developments in the Middle East, the numerous wars, the changes in security measures, the increasing violence and godlessness, the frequent natural disasters—all these could be what Jesus calls "birth pains" (*see* Matthew 24). Unlike the travelers who eagerly observe the signs of fall, many people—even Christians—are oblivious to the signs of the times.

Jesus told a parable about men waiting for their master to return from a banquet. They must be watchful and keep their lamps burning so that they can open the door for him when he returns. Pay attention. Watch and wait. Be ready. Jesus *is* coming again!

"You also must be ready, because the Son of Man will come at an hour when you do not expect him." (Luke 12:40)

PHOTO © Arnold Wheat

THE RIGHT TIME

The farm road on which my friend and I were traveling was deserted. We had gone off the beaten track to look for an antique sale, when a loud bang startled us and our van began to wobble. A blowout! Thankfully, I was able to keep control and pull to the side of the road. I got out and stared at the shredded tire. My friend and I figured we'd have to change it ourselves, a task at which neither of us was particularly adept. I hauled out the lug wrench but couldn't loosens the nuts, even though we took turns jumping up and down on the handle. OK, plan B. Could we drive the van to the nearest town? No, it was at least ten miles away. So, plan C. Was there a house nearby where we could ask to use a phone? Just then a pick-up truck pulled behind us. I felt a bit nervous and vulnerable in our remote location.

"You know, if my wife or daughter was in a fix like this," the pick-up driver said, "I would want a Good Samaritan to stop and help her."

We warily agreed to let him change the tire. But he refused our offer of payment. "It made my day to help some ladies in distress." He certainly had come at just the right time. We were so grateful.

Have you noticed how God provides help at just the right time—perhaps a scripture or encouraging word to buoy your spirit. But sometimes God's right time is not our right time. Remember Lazarus? I'm sure his family did not think Jesus came at the right time. Yet in his time he worked an incredible miracle. Trust God to be there for you and not leave you stranded. He will come.

"We wait in hope for the Lord. He helps us. He is like a shield that keeps us safe." (Psalm 33:20, NlrV)

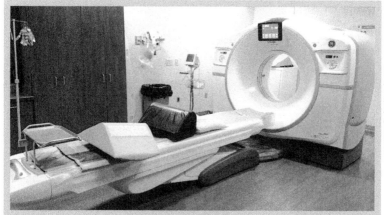

PHOTO © Amber Jones

INCREDIBLE

I injured my shoulder in a fall and had to have an MRI. That machine is incredible! A patient is placed in a tube in which a detailed internal image of a part of the body is produced. According to a hospital brochure I read, an MRI scanner is "a large, powerful magnet where the magnetic field is used to align the magnetization of some atomic nuclei in the body and radio frequency fields to systematically alter the alignment of this magnetization. This causes the nuclei to produce a rotating magnetic field detectable by the scanner—and this information is recorded to construct an image of the scanned area of the body."

Wow. Who comes up with this stuff? MRIs provide good contrast between the different soft tissues of the body, making it superior to X-rays for detecting tears in tendons, muscles and ligaments. As I lay there in this machine, as marvelous as it was, I thought about how much effort, time and noise it takes for men to discover the inner workings of our incredible bodies.

Yet God knows these things more intimately, even from the moment we were conceived. What a great God we have.

> "You shaped me first inside, then out; you formed me in my mother's womb. I thank you, High God—you're breathtaking! Body and soul, I am marvelously made!...You know me inside and out...Like an open book, you watched me grow from conception to birth; all the stages of my life were spread out before you."
> (Psalm 139, The Message)

PHOTO © Susan Roberts

TOO SLOW

The crossing lights flashed and the gates came down. I heard a rumble and a loud horn blast. Oh no, a freight train. The road I take to work crosses a busy railroad track. It seems that on the days I am running late, a slow freight train magically appears, just to mock anyone who's in a rush. It is so hard to wait! I have learned that the best way to cope is to focus on something other than the train. I'll file my nails, make a list, even do exercises. It feels good to accomplish something. When I focus on the train, impatiently drumming my fingers on the steering wheel, time passes at an agonizingly slow pace, and I stress. What if it stops and doesn't get out of the way? How many cars are there anyway? How late am I? However, when I'm otherwise occupied, time passes quickly.

The Bible tells us to wait on God. That's tough. We'll be moving along, and all is fine, and then our road is blocked. We know God is working. But, hey, I've got a problem here and I need an answer! Where are you God? Hurry up! God doesn't want us focusing on this slow train and being filled with worry and impatience. He wants us to fix our eyes on him, exercising faith and practicing trust. We shouldn't miss out on what we could be doing for him because we are so focused on the problem that has gotten in our way.

"I am still confident of this: I will see the goodness of the Lord in the land of the living. Wait for the Lord; be strong and take heart and wait for the Lord."
(Psalm 27:13-14)

PHOTO © CanStockPhoto Inc / Wollwerth

JOG AND JODIES

"I don't know but I've been told..." This is the beginning of a popular "jody" used by the military during physical training. The next line is usually a made-up rhyme of a humorous, challenging, or even off-color nature. This one ends with "...Air Force wings are made of gold."

Designed to grab the soldiers' attention, these jingles help them through the grueling grind of training by keeping their minds off the pain and the long road ahead. When we lived in Hawaii, the troops ran through the housing area shouting their jodies at "o'dark thirty." One challenged: "Lazy wives, get out of bed. Rise and shine you sleepy head." In season, they even chanted Christmas carols to cadence: "I'm. Dreaming. Of a white. Christmas." The resulting camaraderie encourages them to keep going and not give up.

Soldiers learn not to "go it alone" but rely on each other to help them through. Independence is not the best approach for Christians either. We need each other's encouragement. According to the Bible, encouragement helps in battles and provides strength for trials; it inspires good deeds, service and evangelism. Encouragement, friendship, and teamwork not only help us through the tough times, but help us accomplish more. Let's cheer each other on:

I don't know but I've been told ... together we stand strong and bold.
I don't know but what I've heard ... encouragement is a kind word.

"Be devoted to one another in brotherly love. Honor one another above yourselves. Never be lacking in zeal, but keep your spiritual fervor." (Romans 12:10-11)

PHOTO © CanStockPhoto Inc / Aubrey1

NO DANGER

We always chuckle when we drive past some nearby soccer fields, where coyote statues dot the landscape. The intent was to discourage Canada geese from landing and destroying the fields. However, numerous geese are always there, right up close to the "coyotes." The cutouts are certainly not a deterrent. The geese gradually become desensitized to the presence of these stationary predators, learning that they are harmless. We have read that in order to make this tactic effective, the coyote statues need to be moved periodically. Then they will appear to be more of a threat. My husband has often remarked that a smart coyote should stand immovable in the middle of these fake ones. He would then be treated to a banquet of unsuspecting geese.

Our society has gradually become more rude, violent and crass. Things that were not accepted a few years ago are now accepted—bad language, sexual innuendos, graphic violence and dishonest practices. We as Christians may object, but many of us are subtly swept along—maybe not to the extremes—but we certainly are becoming more and more desensitized to the improprieties and sin. We are less shocked. Jesus warned his disciples that the world could be an evil place: Don't allow yourself to become desensitized to evil. Be vigilant. Stand firm.

"I am sending you out like sheep among wolves. Therefore be as shrewd as snakes and as innocent as doves." (Matthew 10:16)

PHOTO © Perry Roberts

A-MAZE-ING

I love the fall season best. I like the crisp days. I like to attend Harvest Festivals, listen to bugling elk, press apple cider and carve pumpkins. A couple of years ago, a group of friends joined me in trying out a corn maze. We laughed and talked as we turned this way and that. Though we found a couple of the punch stations, we became hopelessly lost. Since we didn't know where we were in the first place, our map was useless. All the chatter of well-intentioned advice only confused us more. After a couple of hours we gave up, left the path and cut through the corn stalks, towards the lights of the parking lot. We stumbled some and got scratched, but eventually made it out. Some time later my husband and I visited the same maze with a very conscientious gal who carefully read the map and guided us through the maze, to each punch station and then out, in record time, without distraction. What a difference it made when someone paid attention.

When we get distracted in our spiritual lives, and don't pay attention to God's map, the Bible, or listen to his sound advice, we can become lost also. He wants to guide us on the path we should take, but we make our own way sometimes, stumbling and getting scratched in the process. How blessed we are to have a guide to get us through the maze of life—right up to the end!

"For this God is our God for ever and ever; he will be our guide even to the end."
(Psalm 48:14)

PHOTO © Dr. Daniel Price

THE DIVINE ALCHEMIST

I was not a stellar chemistry student. My lab partner and I fooled around and did not take the class seriously. At one point we took a beaker and mixed the remaining precipitates from an experiment over a Bunsen burner, causing an explosion. Fortunately only the beaker was broken. As you can imagine, this did not sit well with the instructor. We didn't mean to be careless and disrespectful. We simply didn't consider the consequences.

Our missteps and poor choices in life impact the people and situations around us. Often we do not stop and think, but act on the spur of the moment. Things get broken. Relationships with friends and family get compromised. Our reputation may suffer and our trustworthiness diminish. We might be physically or emotionally hurt, or harm another. A scenario that will follow us the rest of our lives may result. We didn't mean this to happen, but Satan gleefully wants to imprison us in the consequences of our sin.

I smiled when I read a quote by Catherine Marshall: "God is the divine Alchemist. He can take junk from the rubbish heap of life and melting this base refuse in the pure fire of his love, hand us back gold."[15] What a joy it is to know that we have been forgiven. Jesus has come to triumph over the destructive efforts of ourselves and Satan, and revive us with a new, abundant life. Don't be discouraged. God can turn anything around and use it for good.

> "The thief comes only to steal and kill and destroy; I have come that they may have life, and have it to the full." (John 10:10)

15. Catherine Marshall, *Moments That Matter* (Nashville: Countryman, 2001).

PHOTO © Pat Burdick

BE WISE

I worked at a high school used textbook sale. As the workers went through the books to determine their condition, we all marveled at the reams of knowledge packed into them. We all agreed that we were glad we were not still in high school. We were significantly intimidated by the pages in the AP Calculus books, not to mention even the tables of contents in the Physics and Chemistry books. There were foreign language books and history books. The English composition book was huge. We had stacks of novels. "Wow, our high-schoolers will be absorbing lots of information. They'll be pretty smart by the end of the year," we thought.

However, smart isn't quite enough. We all have heard about absent-minded professors who have a lot of head knowledge but miss the boat in other ways. God's Word doesn't place much stock in obtaining worldly knowledge. We are told that in comparison to God's wisdom, our wisdom is foolishness. We should strive instead to be filled with the knowledge of God's truth and his will. Solomon, the wisest man ever, says that we should seek wisdom like silver, rubies, or a hidden treasure (see Proverbs 2:4), James tells us if we are lacking in wisdom, we can just ask God (see James 1:5). As the new school year starts let us all "hit the books," learning about God's truth and wisdom, which is far greater than human knowledge and understanding.

"Where is the wise man? Where is the scholar? Where is the philosopher of this age? Has not God made foolish the wisdom of the world?"
(1 Corinthians 1:20)

PHOTO © Dr. John Dennehy

MOUNTAIN HIGH

The peaks were incredibly high and sharp, painted with glaciers and waterfalls. Standing at their base, I felt small and insignificant below the massive, looming mountains. This was the Canadian Rockies near Jasper and Banff National Parks. In contrast, Colorado is already a mile high, so our fourteeners don't seem so daunting; but there at a lower base elevation, the twelve and thirteen-thousand-foot peaks felt overwhelmingly big. As we drove through the high passes, however, we could see seemingly forever—the mountains' mass diminishing behind us as we rose above them.

Our magnificent, huge God has made all this. The Bible says that God formed the mountains by his strength and yet he touches them and they smoke or melt like wax. (*see* Nahum 1:5 and Psalm 97:5). Reflecting on his unmatched creative power in making these massive peaks humbles me. He monitors their very being and they can crumble at the touch of his finger.

I have "mountains" in my own life. Jesus said if we have the faith the size of a mustard seed, we can move mountains. Looking at the size of my personal mountains, it seems impossible. But, nothing is impossible with God. As he, by his Spirit, increases our faith, our view changes. We can see more than the mountain looming. We rise above the problem and the imposing stature melts away. As we trust God, he will indeed move our mountains.

"Because you have so little faith, I will tell you the truth, if you have faith as small as a mustard seed, you can say to this mountain, 'Move from here to there' and it will move. Nothing will be impossible for you." (Matthew 17:20)

PHOTO © Jeff Osterlund

SALT MINES

For miles and miles, all we could see was white. No, not snow. We were passing through Utah's salt flats. Salt is mined here to distribute nationwide. In the ancient world, pure salt was hard to obtain and precious. It was used by royalty and even given to soldiers as wages. Mining salt is an involved process requiring several steps to remove impurities and then add enhancers like anti-clumping ingredients and iodine.

Salt is used to flavor food and also to heal (kill germs), balance bitterness and acidity, preserve from spoilage, and reduce ice and slipperiness. Salt is essential to our bodies as an electrolyte that allows nerve impulses to be transmitted to organs and muscles so that they work efficiently. When our bodies have too little salt, we crave it. Without salt, we would die. On the other hand, too much salt makes food inedible and creates health problems. Salt dumped on the ground stops plant growth and corrodes.

In Matthew's gospel, Jesus compares his followers to salt. Like salt, we are precious and used by royalty! If we lose our saltiness, we lose effectiveness. Neither are we useful if we come on too strong. The Greek word for "losing saltiness" means "foolish or useless." To be fully effective, allow Jesus to remove the impurities in your live. Wise Christians add just the right amount of "spice," not allowing their message to become unpalatable or destructive, but full of joy and pizazz. May our interactions with others be tasteful, healing, and peaceful.

"You are the salt of the earth. But if the salt loses its saltiness, how can it be made salty again?" (Matthew 5:13a)

PHOTO © Mike Kepto

PREPARE FOR THE RACE

The finish line came into view and we cheered wildly as the runner made his final push. He crossed the line—26th out of thousands—in Hawaii's prestigious Iron Man Triathlon. We had flown to Kona, Hawaii to watch this athlete from our alma mater compete. Though we didn't know him, we identified him by the college jersey he wore. The next day at breakfast, we did meet him and learned about his impressive training regimen. He had even written a book about his methods. We were surprised to learn that he had not known how to swim prior to his training, and had to teach himself. Clearly, all his preparations, equipment, diet, training and hard work had paid off.

Any athlete can't just show up and compete. They develop comprehensive training programs where they work out daily, monitor their food and fluid intake, and practice. When they arrive at the starting line, they are well prepared to cross the finish line triumphantly.

We recently attended a musical at Faith Christian Academy. The theme, "Just Run," dramatized the training necessary for our spiritual run. "Coach Q" presented the "3 Qs: Quiet time, no Quitting, and being Quick to listen." A great reminder! When we set apart time for God, he trains us and helps us persevere, even when faith ebbs and odds seem against us. Pastors, teachers and friends can also challenge and encourage us to keep on.

"Do you not know that in a race all the runners run, but only one gets the prize? Run in such a way as to get the prize." (1 Corinthians 9:24)

PHOTO © Susan Roberts

I NEED GAS

Our car needed gas—and soon! We were driving on a remote stretch of highway, no filling stations in sight. We watched anxiously as the gauge moved lower and lower and the fuel light came on. What a relief to finally see a sign for a town with an exit and a gas symbol.

When we travel, we like to keep going; stops for gas seem like an interruption to our time schedule. We probably drive farther than we should before filling up. Our mechanic told us this is not healthy for our car. Driving with a near-empty tank puts undue stress on the fuel pump and can cause it to fail.

We all need spiritual "gas." It's readily available—we don't have to wait for the proper place and time. Our busy lives make us pass by what we desperately need. There comes a point, though, when we are in jeopardy. Our faith wanes, our fears increase, and our ability to operate effectively is compromised. Filling our "tank" with God's Word and presence through prayer and Bible study is a regular spiritual necessity. Take the time to fill up so you can keep going, and run smoothly.

"You made known to me the path of life; you will fill me with joy in your presence, with eternal pleasures at your right hand." (Psalm 16:11)

"May the God of hope fill you with all joy and peace as you trust in him, so that you may overflow with hope by the power of the Holy Spirit." (Romans 15:13)

PHOTO © U.S. Air Force Academy / Charley Starr

YOU CAN DO IT

Driving through Colorado Springs, we passed the Air Force Academy. We began to reminisce about our experiences there. Our son had been a cadet, graduated, and he and his wife were married in the AFA chapel. Our recollections surprised us, though. The more traumatic events took precedence over the proud and joyous occasions. We talked about the difficulties of his Doolie year, and how we had ached for him, prayed for him, and tried to encourage him through all the tough times. He had been injured during Basic and was fighting a bad cold. He was tired and hungry. As parents, we could do very little. Thankfully, God provided strength for him and supplied him with friends who cheered him on. We have often thought that without the encouragement of these fellow cadets, he might not have made it through.

In tough times and daily spiritual battles, we thank God for strength and wisdom. What incredible value we receive through our Christian friends who help us. How thankful we are for their encouragement and prayers. Let us be mindful of praying for one another, encouraging one another, and lend a hand to help in time of need. We echo what Paul wrote to the Colossians:

"[We ask] God to fill you with the knowledge of his will through all spiritual wisdom and understanding. And we pray this in order that you may live a life worthy of the Lord and please him in every way: bearing fruit in every good work, growing in the knowledge of God, being strengthened with all power according to his glorious might so that you may have great endurance and patience." (Colossians 1:9-11)

PHOTO © Susan Roberts

DEEP ROOTS

The recent California drought took a toll on farmers up and down the state. Visiting there, we took an exquisite train ride through the Napa Valley vineyards, past the gorgeous estates of the owners. We asked the tour guide if the California drought was adversely affecting the grape crop. We were surprised when he said that it actually had helped. Wine makers had implemented a technique called "dry farming" in which minimal water is slowly dripped to the plants. The "stress" forces them to send their roots deeper into the ground, and this actually produces a more vigorous plant with sweeter grapes. The drought years have produced some of California's best wines.

Stress can have the same effect on Christians. Although most of us would rather have the comfort of adequate "watering," dry times—when God's living water seems in short supply—force us to send our roots deeper into Christ and depend more wholly on him. Once we do this, we too become "sweeter" and better—stronger and more Christlike. Adversity is never what we would choose, but it does bring about blessings that are above and beyond what one would expect. Let's change our "whine" to "wine"—an outpouring of our spirit that is sweet and rich because of Christ's work in and through us.

"I am the vine; you are the branches. If you remain in me and I in you, you will bear much fruit; apart from me you can do nothing." (John 15:5, NIVUK)

PHOTO © Dr. Ed Holroyd

BUILD ON THE HIGH ROCK

The pelting rain persisted; the rivers swelled. The weather reports warned of flash flooding. The evening news showed scenes of houses and cars submerged or swept along by the currents as rivers surged over their banks. Some folks lost everything. Devastating and terrifying! In many places, only mud, piles of debris, and rising waters could be seen. Our hearts broke for the families who suffered, many confined to inadequate shelters with only basic necessities.

This scene replays throughout our country and the world as storms wreak havoc. Storm surges from the ocean cause similar problems. Homes and businesses along the coasts brace themselves against hurricanes. People often find that their insurance and the government help does not measure up to their expectations. One commentator questioned the wisdom of building in such vulnerable areas—nice places to live when the weather is fine, but a disaster waiting to happen if a storm comes.

Jesus told a parable about building a house on a rock (*see* Matthew 7:23-25). When rains and floods come, they stood firm. It's unwise to build a house on sand. Many of us, though, place our security in "sandy" things of this world like real estate, investments, insurance, authorities, other people, and even ourselves. But when the floods of life eventually come, and these things are diminished, destroyed, or fail to deliver as planned, run to the Lord. He will be your high place where you can stand firm.

"From the ends of the earth I call to you. I call as my heart grows faint; lead me to the rock that is higher than I." (Psalm 61:2)

PHOTO © CanStockPhoto Inc / bereta

THE BIRDS

They swooped in a perfect "V." Their white feathers flashed in the sunlight. The American white pelicans were back. They migrate to our area each spring. We love to watch them fly in formation, floating and banking in unison, and gliding gracefully in to land on the lake. We are sad to see them leave in the fall.

A friend sent us a link to a YouTube video of thousands of starlings flying in unison, making exquisite patterns in the sky. The video explained these flight patterns are called murmerations, and scientists aren't sure why they happen; but they are beautiful.

One time we saw nearby trees filled with noisy birds. They didn't fly with grace and unity. Startled, they took to the air in mass confusion. What a haphazard swarm compared to the beauty of unity.

When Christians come together to work in unison, it is also beautiful. As one body, we can move together to create something wonderful, reflecting the Son. Before his death, Jesus prayed: "I have given them the glory that you gave me, that they may be one as we are one—I in them and you in me-so that they may be brought to complete unity. Then the world will know that you sent me and have loved them even as you have loved me" (John 17:22, NIVUK). Let's not do our own thing with noise and confusion. Let's work together to display something beautiful.

"Make every effort to keep the unity of the Spirit through the bond of peace. Be completely humble and gentle; be patient, bearing with one another in love."
(Ephesians 4:3-2, NIVUK)

PHOTO © Larry Lawton

CAST SHEEP

Our granddaughter brought home a multi-colored tissue paper sheep she had made in Sunday School. She called it Dipping Dots because the dotted colors resembled that sweet treat. We quizzed her about her lesson and discovered her class was studying sheep. They learned about their characteristics, how we are like them, and how our Good Shepherd Jesus protects and cares for us. This particular lesson was about "cast sheep." We had never heard of them, so we asked her to explain. A sheep that has rolled onto its back and can't get up is called a cast. This happens most commonly with short, stocky sheep that have full, dirty fleeces. Sheep get tired and lie down. In their effort to get comfortable, they may roll onto their backs. Cast sheep can become distressed and die within a short period of time if they are not rolled back into a normal position. Gases of its stomach build up in its rumen and the pressure cuts off circulation. The blood cannot do its job. But when the sheep calls out, the shepherd comes to its aid. Once rescued, it may need to be carried while it regains steadiness.

We are like sheep. We wander off, away from the Shepherd. Our independence makes us tired. We get ourselves into trouble. We are over laden with burdens and the weight of dirty sin. We try to rest, try to get comfortable, but become cast. When we call out to Jesus, his forgiveness and renewal sets us right again. Peter tells us that we are like sheep gone astray, but we have returned to the shepherd who is the overseer of our souls (*see* 1 Peter 2:25).

"Answer me, O Lord, out of the goodness of your love...Come near and rescue me: for I am in trouble." (Psalm 69:16-18)

PHOTO © CanStockPhoto Inc / JohnNorth

NECESSARY SUPPLIES

When we lived in Hawaii, powerful hurricane Ewa hit us directly, on the day before Thanksgiving. Before the hurricane's landfall, we were warned to stock up on essentials. Loss of power and limited travel ability were expected. I left our toddlers with a sitter and took off to purchase batteries, charcoal, bottled water, and other supplies. The stores had sold out. After several stops, I finally found a 7-11 with a few batteries and some other necessities—not all I needed, but at least some. I got back to the worried sitter just as the wind began to pick up. I then hurried to board up our windows and take the recommended precautions. The storm hit with full force. We were without power for ten days and without water for five. Thankfully, we were safe. We spent Thanksgiving with our neighbors, cleaning out our unusable refrigerators and freezers, and cooking out on barbecue grills.

God's supplies never run out. He offers limitless grace, love and forgiveness. The Israelites sinned against God over and over again, yet he continued to love them, forgive them and provide for their needs. I can identify with them. I too fail God over and over, yet he continues to be faithful, and his mercies never cease. He is willing to provide just what we need, and he is our strong fortress in the storm. Praise God for his unfailing love!

"Because of the Lord's great love, we are not consumed, for his compassions never fail. They are new every morning; great is your faithfulness. I say to myself, 'The Lord is my portion; therefore I will wait for him.'" (Lamentations 3:22-24)

PHOTO © CanStockPhoto Inc / dariolopresti

ANTS

I decided to follow King Solomon's advice in Proverbs 6:6, to consider the ant and be wise. So I researched ants and was surprised to learn that most species hibernate—only one kind actually collects food for the winter. Ants are truly remarkable in other ways, as well. Their highly socialized colony designates soldiers/protectors, builders, movers, nursery workers, food gatherers/preparers, queen attendants, guides, and trash collectors. They work as a well-coordinated team, filling in and helping each other with the tasks at hand. They rescue and care for injured ants. They leave scent trails to guide others to food and safety. They even have two stomachs—one for digesting their own food, and one for storing food for others. How incredible!

We can indeed learn wisdom from ants. As a Christian body, we too can help each other and work as a unified team to accomplish the tasks at hand.

After my surgery, my husband and I were the grateful and amazed recipients of an incredible outpouring of love and caring as folks prayed, called, sent cards, brought meals, did errands and chores for us. Furthermore, we often see people in our church coming together to work as a team to provide and prepare food, take care of the young and sick, build, clean up, and serve. Surely God is pleased!

"We will grow to become in every respect the mature body of him who is the head, that is, Christ. From him the whole body, joined and held together by every supporting ligament, grows and builds itself up in love, as each part does its work." (Ephesians 4:15-16)

PHOTO © Dr. Ed Holroyd

REFLECTIONS

There wasn't even a ripple. The wind was still and the pond was as smooth as glass. Mountains, trees, sky and clouds reflected on the quiet water. A wood duck perched on a tree stump, sitting as motionless as the pool below, his image mirrored on the surface. A breeze came up and his feathers ruffled as his image disappeared from the broken waters. Off he flew, as if the disturbance had reminded him of places he needed to visit.

When we are quiet and receptive, we can hear God's voice, receive his prompting and be renewed in our inner being. This enables us to project his image to those around us. The challenge is to keep reflecting even when there is a disturbance. Are we worried about what is happening? Are we distracted by the things we need to accomplish? Can we still stop and pay attention to God? If our hearts are pure and steadfast, unruffled because of the work of the Spirit in our lives, we can project tranquility out of the depth of our hearts in spite of the turbulence that tries to fluster us. "As the water reflects a face, so a man's heart reflects a man" (Proverbs 27:19). It is not what is on the outside that determines our response, but what is on the inside. Let us look to God for inner strength. We need him. Don't let the winds of fate ruffle your reflection. He alone can temper our hearts so that we continually reflect his peace.

"The Lord looks deep down inside every heart. He understands every desire and every thought. If you look to him, you will find him." (1 Chronicles 28:9, NIrV)

PHOTO © Dr. Ed Holroyd

SNAKE IN THE GARDEN

Our grandson came rushing into the house, nearly out of breath. "Grandma, Grandma," he shouted. He had been out by our rose garden and had discovered a small snake curled up inside a cinder block. We watched as the snake glided out and disappeared in the foliage. We looked up pictures of snakes on the internet and identified it as a Western Terrestrial Garter Snake. I'm glad we didn't try to pick it up. Although it doesn't have a poisonous bite, its saliva can be quite harmful.

My grandson's excitement at discovering something in nature reminded me of a recent Genesis study about the pleasure God had taken in creation. "God saw it was very good" (Genesis 1:31). I'm sure God is delighted when we discover and get excited about some aspect of what he has made. How many times I have worked in the garden and not noticed things around me—this little guy was probably right under my nose. Sometimes it takes the eyes of a child to help us see.

Do take time to "smell the roses." God has awesome things to show us right under our noses if we will only take the time to see.

"The earth is the Lord's, and its fullness, the world and those who dwell therein...Lift up your heads, O you gates! And be lifted up, you everlasting doors; and the King of Glory shall come in. Who is this King of Glory? The Lord of hosts, he is the King of Glory." (Psalm 24:1, 9-10, NKJV)

PHOTO © Susan Roberts

IN EVERY SEASON

A beautiful maple tree grows in our front yard. Passersby even stop to photograph it. In the fall its leaves turn brilliant red. As we drive up to our house, it inspires us to praise our almighty Creator. We also love it in the spring when lacy leaves appear, and in the summer when it provides cool shade. Now as it drops leaves, exposing naked branches, it is not so great to see. The falling leaves require lots of yard clean-up; so far we have raked up almost 20 trash bags of leaves. We don't look forward to the hard, continual work. Even so, we don't love the tree less. We know its wonderful potential.

At times we are reminded of our imperfections. Our ugly side becomes exposed for all to see. Like Adam and Eve, we try to hide our ugliness or failures, but God sees through our "leaves" to the nakedness of our sin. Truly it is wonderful how he loves us anyway. He knows our potential and, because of Jesus, is willing to forgive us, clean us up, and be patient while we become what he knows we can be. "Praise the Lord, my soul and forget not his benefits—who forgives all your sins" (Psalm 103:2-3).

We can apply this principle to our dealings with others: forgiving as God has forgiven us; being patient and loving with people even when their ugly side is exposed, knowing they have incredible potential.

"Love keeps no record of wrongs, thinks no evil, does not rejoice in iniquity, but rejoices in the truth; bears all things, believes all things, hopes all things, endures all things. Love never fails." (1 Corinthians 13:5-8)

PHOTO © Susan Roberts

ABUNDANT FRUIT

That was a year of bountiful fruit crops. As we drove around town, we saw lots of trees laden with apples, cherries, peaches, and pears that were falling to the ground unused. I wished I could take a wheelbarrow and run all over town collecting the unused drops and put them to good use—breads, pies, sauces, juices, dried and canned fruits—so many possibilities! Food banks and needy folks could use these too! What a shame to see the fruit just lying there rotting and going to waste.

According to Galatians chapter five, the Holy Spirit develops the fruit of the Spirit in us. Through him, we have the abundant use of love, joy, peace, patience, kindness, goodness, faithfulness, gentleness, and self control. By God's grace, we are laden with fruit. But is it languishing, hidden as if behind a backyard fence, unused?

If we are not serving in God's kingdom, or if we fail to connect in meaningful ways with his people, our fruit goes to waste. In Matthew 25 Jesus told a parable about a landowner who went on a journey and entrusted money to his servants. Some put what they received to good use. Others did not. When the master returned he was displeased with those who had not wisely used what they had been given. Don't let what you've been given go to waste. What are you doing to use your fruit? Let us use what we have, so someday God will say:

> "Well done, good and faithful servant! You have been faithful with a few things. I will put you in charge of many things. Come and share your master's happiness." (Matthew 25:21)

PHOTO © Susan Roberts

TOMATO CAGES

I can hardly wait for my garden tomatoes to ripen. The thought of one sliced on my plate makes my mouth water. My grandkids call the cherry tomatoes "garden candy." We plant plenty of tomatoes each spring, placing the baby plants inside large wire cages. At first they seem dwarfed, but soon the leggy plants spread this way and that. All summer I trim them and stick the branches back into the cage, lest the whole thing topple over. The plant is much more fruitful when it stands up tall, exposed to sunlight. All the work and anticipation are rewarded come fall, when we harvest tomatoes.

In Bible study we learned that Daniel stood up with courage for what he believed, even under the threat of death. Though he and his people were exiled to Babylon, he didn't forsake his God by adopting the practices of his new country. He was not standing alone. God was his strength and helper as he prayed daily, and his friends also prayed fervently for him (*see* Daniel 2:18). He confidently anticipated the great things God would do.

As Christians, we find ourselves in a Babylon of godlessness. We need to stand for righteousness but cannot do it alone. Like Daniel, we must pray daily and trim away the weight of sin and distractions that could pull us down. To keep from falling, we need to share our struggles with others and allow them to surround and support us with prayer. Then, like Daniel, we can confidently anticipate the great things God will do.

> "Prayer is essential in this ongoing warfare. Pray hard and long. Pray for your brothers and sisters..." (Ephesians 6:18, The Message)

PHOTO © Brooke Roberts

PICKING PUMPKINS

Crazy Colorado! Fall is supposed to be chilly, but some days are surprisingly warm, then snow can come a few days later. The weather report predicted one of these dramatic temperature swings, so in preparation for the frost and cold, I gathered up the grandkids and we headed to the garden to pick pumpkins. We lugged them up our backyard hill, then up the steps to the house. We huffed and puffed with our heavy loads, happy to finally reach our destination and set them down. Whew! I was glad for the help.

We each carry burdens that often feel heavy. Dealing with life's issues can be an uphill battle. What a relief to have help. Friends and family may be there for us. This old hymn reminds us that Jesus wants to carry our burdens:

> What a friend we have in Jesus, all our sins and grief to bear.
> What a privilege to carry, everything to God in prayer.
> Oh what peace we often forfeit. Oh what needless pain we bear.
> All because we do not carry everything to God in prayer.

Let us carry our burdens to Jesus and experience the sweet relief of setting them down. We do not have to lug them around by ourselves, experiencing weariness and pain. We do have the wonderful privilege of coming to God in prayer, knowing that he indeed will hear and answer.

"Praise be to the Lord, to God our Savior, who daily bears our burdens."
(Psalm 68:19)

PHOTO © Susan Roberts

SWEET AROMA

I walked into the kitchen from the blustery outside and was met with the pleasing aroma of fresh-baked cookies. That cinnamon-sweet smell is one of my favorite parts of fall, especially on chilly days. That inviting fragrance makes me want to walk right in, sit right down, put up my feet and sample the tasty treats, accompanied by a cup of cocoa.

When we had our house on the market, the realtor suggested baking cookies before a showing. If time is short, even boiling water with cinnamon can have a similar effect, making the house more appealing and welcoming, helping the sale.

The Bible says that we can be a pleasing aroma to those around us. A positive attitude, a cheerful smile, a kind word can make people feel welcome and wanted. It can open the door to share the love of Jesus. What can we do to welcome people into our churches? They need a safe haven from the storms outside and a place where they can feel at home. What can we do in our neighborhoods? Have we extended warm invitations and are our doors open to welcome visitors? When folks come in, it is our prayer that they will sense the sweet aroma of Jesus in us and feel welcomed to walk right in, sit right down, put up their feet and taste and see the goodness of our Lord (*see* Psalm 34:8).

"For we are to God the pleasing aroma of Christ among those who are being saved and those who are perishing." (2 Corinthians 2:15)

PHOTO © Susan Roberts

THERE'S AN APP FOR THAT

"There's an app for that." Cell phone apps are available for about anything one can imagine. Our kids have been showing us some of these incredible offers, available either for free or for purchase. Our daughter has an app that will alert her to stores in her vicinity that have specials or available coupons. She can also scan an item's bar code, find where it is sold nearby, and compare prices. Another app allows you to point your phone at the stars and identify the constellations. Our favorite app is the GPS and direction map. We can plan a route and know how long it will take, find out where traffic snarls and accidents are, and even have a pleasant voice guide us to our destination. However, though our kids use the apps easily, we are finding that it takes some training and knowledge to know what is available and to use it effectively.

What if we had an app to connect with God? Just point your phone at the heavens and put in requests, receive answers and directions, and get instant help, healing and wisdom—whatever is needed. Instead, we have prayer. Prayer is available at any time without cost. We can ask God anything. But, it is not quite that easy. We must train our minds to hear his voice and respond to his Spirit. We often need to wait on his timing. Things don't happen instantly. We also are subject to God's will, which might not be to our liking at the moment. Yet, we have access to the Almighty God and can come boldly before him with our petitions. He loves us, hears us, helps us, and knows what is best for us.

"If you remain in me and my words remain in you, ask whatever you wish and it will be given." (John 15:17)

PHOTO © Susan Roberts

PRESSING MATTERS

I have a friend who loves to iron. Not me. If I can't just fluff it up in the dryer, the garment doesn't get worn. My ironing basket is full of items waiting for attention. Ironing to me is one of those unfulfilling tasks that moments later needs repeating. My friend disagrees. She thinks pressing clothes is therapeutic—it's great to smooth things over and remove the wrinkles, making the clothes crisp and neat. For her, it is not work, but a joy.

Taking care of pressing matters is another thing altogether. Perhaps there are some pressing tasks we need to do for God's kingdom. These should not be ignored, but need our prompt attention. There are people and situations in all of our lives that need a warm and caring touch. We might need to smooth things over in a relationship. We might need to help someone through the "wrinkles" in their lives that cause them distress. Jesus said that when we do something for others, it is like we are doing it for him (*see* Matthew 25:45), and we are stacking up lasting treasure in heaven that can't be destroyed.

This does take time—just a casual "fluffing" might not be enough. We may need to apply ourselves intentionally to the task at hand. We should take on God's kingdom work, not grudgingly, but with joy.

"I press on toward the goal to win the prize for which God has called us heavenward in Christ Jesus." (Philippians 3:14)

PHOTO © Susan Roberts

CLOGGED

Guests were coming. I was in a hurry and stuffed way too many potato peels down my garbage disposal. Yes, you guessed it! I ended up with a gargantuan clog, requiring plumber assistance. Water was backed up and the sink would not drain. This, of course, kept the disposal from doing its job, and made entertaining and serving my guests difficult.

I know destructive things happen when I am in a hurry, especially in my spiritual life. The "pipeline" to God becomes clogged when busyness or sins get in the way. This limits the flow of God's power and Spirit that I need, and I am not fully receptive to God's voice and leading. Then I'm not effective as a Christian.

If we want to be conduits of God's love to the world around us, our pipeline to God's love and power must be kept wide open, allowing God's love to freely flow through us to others. Time spent in prayer and Bible study helps us keep the channel open to God's voice and the power of his Spirit.

Jesus offers us living water, which is the Holy Spirit. We need this power, peace, love, and discernment. If we keep our pipeline open and get rid of the garbage, living water can flow freely through us to others. Then we will be effective servants, doing the job God has called us to do.

"If anyone is thirsty, let him come to me and drink....Whoever believes in me...streams of living water will flow from within him." (John 7:38)

PHOTO © CanStockPhoto Inc / liveslow

APPRECIATE THE SACRIFICE

Dust storms and desert heat. Separated families and danger. Long hours and hard work both for families at home and for those deployed. Our brave men and women fight on foreign soil so that our homeland may be secure from those who would destroy it. Unfortunately, "there's a peace only to be found on the other side of war" (as Sean Connery's character said in the movie, *First Knight*). As long as there are those who care nothing for peace, we must hold on to our resolve and make it impossible for them to succeed. We're thankful for military men and women and their families, who willingly sacrifice to serve our country. They have not chosen an easy road, yet their efforts are paramount in preserving our freedom, protecting us from harm, and securing peace. Let us solemnly cheer them on, appreciating the sacrifices they make in both life and death.

Many others make sacrifices, too, willingly placing themselves in harm's way, leaving friends and family, and often working at hard, thankless tasks. Missionaries and church planters, as well as police and firemen should also be recipients of our appreciation.

We have all been called to serve and sacrifice. We might not be called to foreign lands and dangerous situations, or to leave friends and family, but we are called to leave our comfort zone and serve Jesus no matter what the cost. He gave everything for us, and he requires everything from us.

"If anyone would come after me, he must deny himself and take up his cross daily and follow me." (Luke 9:23)

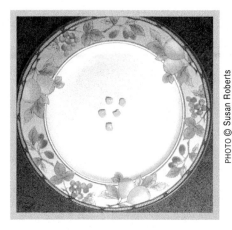

PHOTO © Susan Roberts

FIVE KERNELS OF CORN

The turkey was stuffed and roasted to a golden brown. All the side dishes—green bean casserole, mashed potatoes, and assorted vegetables were piping hot. They sent enticing aromas into the dining room from the kitchen. The salads and cranberry sauce waited on the counter, along with the relish tray. There was enough food to feed "army." As they gathered, the family took their places at the festive, beautifully-set table. But they could not eat just yet. There, sitting on each plate, were five kernels of cooked corn.

What in the world? I'm hungry. Let's eat. The food is getting cold.

These kernels are an important part of our Thanksgiving celebration, though. They represent the Pilgrims' second Thanksgiving. The colonists were feeling pretty smug and self sufficient after their first bountiful harvest. God's generosity and care was soon forgotten. A winter of want sent them to their knees, confessing their sin and imploring the Lord to help and provide. They were rationed to five kernels of corn each per day. Somehow, through a series of miracles, God helped them through and all of them survived. They remembered that it was God who had done this, not themselves. They began their second Thanksgiving with five kernels of corn to remind them of the faithful provision of Jehovah Jirah, the God who provides. It is not our efforts which have accomplished the bounty of our table, but God. Let us solemnly thank him.[16]

"Command those who are rich in this present world not to be arrogant nor put their hope in wealth, which is so uncertain, but to put their hope in God who richly provides us with everything for our enjoyment." (1 Timothy 6:17)

16. Recounted in: Peter Marshall and David Manuel, *The Light and the Glory* (Revell, 2009).

PHOTO © Kirk Dorn

CARAMEL APPLES

After Halloween, we noticed stores had caramel apples on sale. They looked fine, but the apples inside had gotten mushy and spoiled. They soon disappeared from the shelves. No one really wants to buy an apple that looks good but is rotten at the core.

When Israel wanted a king, Samuel warned it was not in their best interest. He eventually anointed Saul, who was an impressive young man. Saul did not obey God's precepts, and God soon rejected him as king. Samuel then went to Jesse's sons in search of a new king. He was impressed with Abinadab and thought surely he must be God's choice. God reminded him: "Do not consider his appearance or his height….The Lord does not look at the things man looks at. Man looks at the outward appearance, but the Lord looks at the heart" (1 Samuel 16:7). Eventually David, Jesse's youngest, was chosen to be king.

In our nation, we have the precious freedom of voting for our leaders. Let us take this responsibility solemnly and not refrain from voting because candidates are not to our liking. When we choose, be careful to not look just at appearances. Good looks and smooth talk may sway many in their votes. Instead, seek God for wisdom and pray that other voters will be wise as well. May God's justice in deterring voter fraud, and his mercy in providing for the best leaders for this nation, be realized. Pray that God's best choice for this nation, and not our misguided desires, will prevail. May God bless America.

> "Everyone must submit himself to the governing authorities, for there is no authority except that which God has established." (Romans 13:1)

PHOTO © Carol Cassell

HAPPY BIRTHDAY TO ME

Our grandkids enjoy every minute of birthday celebrations: the presents, candles, cake, and balloons. They each get to pick their party theme. Our granddaughter loves princesses. For days our three-year-old grandson, anticipating his big day, went around the house loudly singing "Happy birthday to me." Sometimes circumstances allow us to have numerous celebrations for a birthday with different family members and friends. That is quite all right with the kids. After each party they ask, "When can I do it again?"

As we get older, birthdays lose some of their charm. Birthday cards caustically catalogue all the woes of wrinkles, sags, and memory loss of old age. Getting old is not for sissies! Many of us would just as soon forget the day.

Each of us, if we believe in Jesus, has a spiritual birthday when we were reborn into God's family. At first we were enthused and joyfully exercised our newfound faith. We were attuned to all the wonderful gifts God had given us. As we continue in our Christian walk, however, we may lose some of that joy. Perhaps we become calloused, tired, and bogged down with burdens. Our faith fades into practicality and self sufficiency. God's Good News becomes old news and Bible reading redundant. We forget all of God's greatness. No wonder the church in Ephesus was told not to forsake their first love (*see* Revelation 2:4).

God's Spirit in us can renew and revive, lightening our hearts. Focusing on God with thankfulness and praise sets us free from the doldrums. Remember your wonderful spiritual birthday and joyfully sing, "Happy birthday to me."

"Restore to me the joy of your salvation." (Psalm 51:12)

PHOTO © Perry Roberts

PASS IT ON

What has your family passed on from generation to generation? The first thing that comes to mind in our family is soccer. Although my husband and I never played ourselves, our enthusiasm for the sport has been carried on to our kids and grandkids. Our family also loves to play games. I learned my first card game from my grandmother. We played often with my parents, and now we continue with our kids and their kids. Another legacy that has been continued is the importance and sanctity of marriage. My grandparents were married for over sixty years, as were my parents. My husband and I have topped forty-four, and we are thrilled that our kids also have enduring marriages.

None of these are of utmost importance though. Beginning with my parents, a life-changing legacy began. My mom accepted Jesus when she was an adult, and that was passed on to her kids. Now, we have in turn passed our belief in God and his Word on to our children. It is a thrill to see our grandchildren pick up this torch, accept Jesus as their Savior and honor God in their lives. It is true that parents cannot always influence the paths their kids will take. Many great Bible patriarchs have had children that didn't follow the Lord. It is only God's grace in answer to prayers that allows this. Keeping the truth of the Lord in the forefront of our homes is the most important thing we can do to continue a legacy. Pass it on. This is our best investment for the future.

"Fix these words of mine in your hearts and minds...Teach them to your children, talking about them as you sit at home and when you walk along the road, when you lie down and when you get up." (Deuteronomy 11:18-19)

PHOTO © Brooke Roberts

DISSENTING VOICE

We took a fall outing with a group of friends. Exuberantly, we shared what we loved about fall: wonderful sights of colored leaves, corn stalks, pumpkins, and scarecrows; tantalizing smells of log fires, cider, and pies baking; our favorite fall foods like caramel apples, cocoa, pumpkin bread, and candy; the touch of chill lingering beneath the warm sun; fun times of hayrides, corn mazes, and jumping in freshly raked leaves; bountiful harvests of fruits, tomatoes, squashes, and pumpkins, which inspired baking and canning.

But as our group of friends shared their fondness for fall, there was one dissenting voice. "I do not like fall," one gentleman said. "The days get too short and I miss the evening light. The cool air reminds me that winter is coming and I don't like navigating in snow and ice. I don't like sweets, squash or pumpkin." OK, there's an Eeyore in every group.

It is amazing how that one dissenting voice took the wind out of everyone's sails, though. Their happiness balloons popped. The Bible says, "a little leaven leavens the whole lump of dough" (1 Corinthians 5:6, NASB). Let us be careful not to be the leaven of hopelessness, defeat, discontentment or negativity. Let us instead make every effort to share the fruits of righteousness, joy, love and peace. Positive attitudes are not only helpful to those we meet, but healing to our own spirit also.

"Pleasant words are a honeycomb, sweet to the soul and healing to the bones." (Proverbs 16:24)

PHOTO © Charissa McCaslin

ALL IS WORSHIP

When our son was a high school senior, he was the captain of the soccer team at a Christian high school. In a pre-season retreat the team decided to focus the entire season on honoring God in every way, every time they stepped on the pitch (field). They believed that to do their very best was a way to worship God through playing soccer. When a goal was scored, they all pointed heavenward, giving the glory to God. They prayed that their attitudes and conduct towards the referees and the other players would be exemplary, doing what God would have them do. They thanked God for every opportunity, whether it was successful or not.

Their example taught us that worship is not just singing in church or praying. We can worship God in everything we do from the most mundane task to the most difficult challenge by doing it for him. Colossians 3:23, 24 says: "Whatsoever you do, do it heartily, as to the Lord, and not unto men; knowing that of the Lord you shall receive the reward of the inheritance: for you serve the Lord Jesus Christ." The Soccer team went on to win the state championship. They made a highlight video of their soccer season with background music of "Here I am to Worship." No matter what you are doing today, start by saying, "Here I am to worship" and do everything to the honor and glory of God!

"May you always be doing those good, kind things that show you are a child of God, for this will bring much praise and glory to the Lord." (Philippians 1:11, TLB)

PHOTO © Carol Cassell

PICK UP YOUR EQUIPMENT

Piles of supplies were spread out on our family-room floor: notebooks and folders, pencils, pens and markers, lined and plain paper, glue and tape. We had just returned from the store where we had purchased all the items on the list of supplies needed to start school. The kids are enrolled, and have their class lists and teachers' names. Now the kids are packing their backpacks with everything they will need. Some of their specialized classes require additional equipment: gym shoes for PE, a graphing calculator for math, instruments for music, head phones for computer lab. Soon they will be learning new skills and studying, fully prepared for any challenge in every course.

When we enrolled in God's family, by accepting Jesus as our Savior, it became time to start "school." We are learning to know God and his Word and studying so that we will be able to correctly handle his truth (*see* 2 Timothy 2:15). The Bible is our prime textbook. We need specialized equipment too. We must be prepared to combat Satan's attacks that would put us off course. God's equipment is free by his grace. We do not have to buy it or earn it. We just have to pick it up. We can put on his full armor: the belt of truth, the sword of the Spirit—God's Word, the breastplate of righteousness, the shield of faith, the helmet of salvation and the shoes of the gospel of peace (*see* Ephesians 6:10-17). Fill your backpack with all that you'll need, so you'll be prepared for every challenge.

"His divine power has given us everything we need for life and godliness."
(2 Peter 1:3)

PHOTO © Carol Cassell

KNOWING THE RULES

I don't know much about football. My husband usually has to explain to me what's happening. That is not the case with the "other football" (soccer). We've taken classes, refereed, coached, watched our kids play; and now we watch our grandkids play.

When our granddaughter was eight, she had a Saturday soccer match. She had advanced to playing on a large field with big goals. The referee thought it was time they learned the rules of the game, so he started calling "off sides," one of the more difficult rules of soccer. Every time the whistle blew and play was stopped, the girls turned and asked, "What?" They were clueless. The parents were clueless too. Some of us tried to explain the call, but they still didn't get it. It was difficult for the girls to follow a rule that they didn't understand. Whether or not they understood, though, with every violation of the rule, the girls were penalized.

Paul's epistle to the Romans tells us God's law used to be so lengthy and difficult to understand that no one could follow it. But that was the point. God's law exists to show us our inadequacy and need of a Savior. We are helpless to follow the laws, but Jesus has redeemed us by his grace. If we believe, confess, and turn from sin, we can enter his "game" confident that he has justified us and will not penalize us.

> "...No one will be declared righteous in his sight by observing the law; rather, through the law we become conscious of sin. But now a righteousness from God, apart from the law, has been made known...This righteousness from God comes through faith in Jesus Christ to all who believe." (Romans 3:20-22)

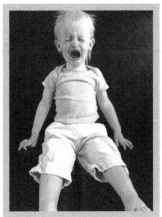

PHOTO © Dr. Michelle Williamson

"NO!" OR "YES!"?

"No!" This is one of the first words a toddler learns, and she'll generally use it often to limit what she'll do, what she'll wear, what she'll eat and where she'll go. Usually she is overruled by adults in her life who know what is best for her.

Sometimes the limits set by "No" are good. Remember the "Just Say No" campaign by Nancy Reagan to combat drug abuse? We certainly want to say, "No" to dangerous, destructive and unhealthy temptations. Yet, sometimes we say "No" to things that are beneficial. God occasionally calls us to do things that are out of our comfort zone. Service needs in our church, community, and world might seem scary, inconvenient, or distasteful. Are we in the habit of saying "No" and setting limits on what God can do in and through us?

We listened to a speaker who told about a commitment he had made to say "yes" to God. He would not argue about it, worry about, it or go in a different direction. His experiences were wild and crazy and he was stretched to his limits, but he did some things that many would say were impossible. God was faithful in everything, and he was exhilarated by the magnitude of God's actions.

Are you ready to say "Yes!" to God? Are you ready to smash the limits and walk by faith? Do you want to lead a dynamic Christian life propelled by yeses? What is God calling you to do? Make a transfer of power from your "No" to God's "Yes." You will be amazed at what happens and how you are blessed.

"I pray that the eyes of your heart may be enlightened in order that you may know the hope to which he has called you, the riches of his glorious inheritance in the saints, and his incomparably great power for us who believe." (Ephesians 1:18-19)

PHOTO © Chris Head

SUPER HEROES

What kid doesn't like to pretend to be a super hero? I was surprised to discover that there are real-life super heroes. Apparently an international registry exists for people who wish to adopt an alternative persona and enter the realm of rogue crime fighting, environmental protection, and political activism, wearing a costume and mask. Here's what one superhero from Utah had to say: "I wear a uniform with a mask. I may be a bit odd by normal standards but, like so many others in the world today, I saw a need for change. So, I started within myself. That's when wearing the uniform, and patrolling the city at night became my other job." Another from California writes: "I work to help make a difference by doing civic activities, crime fighting and charity work. My main objective is to inspire others."

Many of us do notice a need for change in the world around us. As hard as we try, man's best efforts are insufficient. Only God can change hearts and make things new, clean and right. God is much more than a super hero. We do have the capacity to change the world in supernatural ways, but not by our own initiative. We are the hands and feet of God, doing his bidding. We work for God with God.

"For when you did awesome things that we did not expect, you came down, and the mountains trembled before you. Since ancient times no one has heard, no ear has perceived, no eye has seen any God besides you, who acts on behalf of those who wait for him." (Isaiah 64:3-4)

PHOTO © Susan Roberts

EARS TO HEAR

How many times have we told our kids to clean their rooms? We expect them to do it right away. How frustrating it would be if they came back in a couple of hours and said, "I heard every word. I memorized what you said. I can even say it in Hebrew and Greek!" Or, maybe they might remark, "I contemplated what you said and I think I really have a handle on it. I even invited over some friends to talk about the best ways to get it done, and we developed a strategy."

None of this gets the job done. We just want them to clean their rooms. Period.

In Francis Chan's *Basic* series,[17] he teaches on this subject. He says God has given us his commands in his Word, and we often just memorize them, contemplate them, or discuss them; but we don't *do* them. We aren't even in the same boat as Jonah who willfully disobeyed; but we, too, don't get the job done. It is important to listen to God's Word, but it is even more important to put his words and will into action. Let's seek to be effective followers of Jesus and do his bidding.

"Do not merely listen to the word, and so deceive yourselves. Do what it says. Anyone who listens to the Word but does not do what it says is like man who looks at his face in a mirror and, after looking at himself, goes away and immediately forgets what he looks like." (James 1:22-24)

17. http://basicseries.com/

PHOTO © Larry Lawton

PLAYGROUND

Swing on the swings, go down the slides, cross the monkey bars, climb on the ladder—We have fun taking our grandkids to the playground and watching them play and learn new skills. They often will watch other kids and copy what they are doing. Some of the things they've learned were helpful and imaginative. They've learned to try something new and not be afraid. Other ideas were dangerous or beyond their skill level, but they've wanted to try them nonetheless, so we remain vigilant. The biggest challenge has been preventing them from imitating the kids who don't follow the rules: climbing the slide the wrong way, throwing rocks and mulch, pushing and bullying and not waiting their turns. At one point, we even had to leave a playground because of multiple bad influences.

We, as God's children, should also be influenced by good examples. We are told to follow Jesus, not the evil ways of the world. Don't be persuaded by false teachers or destructive practices. Be discerning and flee from what is evil. Don't imitate those who would lead you astray (*see* 1 Timothy 4:1, 2 Peter 2:2, Jude 1:16).

Godly people can be models for us to imitate. They can encourage us to try new things, to behave in a godly way and to be inspired in our Christian life. Make sure you follow those who follow Jesus.

"Dear friends, do not imitate what is evil but what is good. Anyone who does what is good is from God. Anyone who does what is evil has not seen God." (3 John 1:11)

PHOTO © Susan Roberts

HOW LONG CAN YOU HOLD ON?

My psychologist friend gave a seminar on stress. In her hand she held a partially-full glass of water. People expected her to talk about the half-full/half empty analogy. Instead, she asked the audience how much they thought the glass weighed. People suggested 8 oz., 12 oz., etc. The speaker held the glass out in her hand and explained that it was light and easy to hold. However, after several minutes, it began to feel heavy. She explained that her hand and arm were becoming tired and painful cramps were starting. If she held it for an hour, her shoulder and neck would cramp, her arm would go numb. Holding it for a day was almost impossible.

That's the way with worry. At first our worry seems small; but the longer we hold it, the more it debilitates. Physical issues may develop—upset stomach, ulcers, headaches, high blood pressure and even illnesses. Attitude issues may surface—crankiness, depression, anger, and a critical spirit. Peter tells us to cast all our cares on Jesus, for he cares for us (*see* 1 Peter 5:7). Thank God ahead of time for his answers to your problems, then release them to him. Then you don't have to bother with them anymore. Make each day a praying day. Intercede for the needs of others. Problems are opportunities for creative solutions, and a chance to see God at work. God will give hope, help, and peace.

> "Do not be anxious about anything, but in every situation, by prayer and petition, with thanksgiving, present your requests to God. And the peace of God, which transcends all understanding, will guard your hearts and your minds in Christ Jesus." (Philippians 4:6-7)

ACKNOWLEDGEMENTS

Many people came together to help launch this book. I am so grateful to God for this "army" He created to help fulfill each need. I want to offer special thanks to Jeff and Jana Osterlund who posed, photographed and encouraged me through this process. Also special thanks to Kirk and Marilee Dorn who went out of their way to take pictures and stayed up late proofing everything at the last minute. Kent and Donna Nelson were also an incredible help with photography and encouragement. I would like to do a shout out to all the caring, wonderful people who have read the Arvada Covenant Church Prayer Line, and have encouraged this project from the beginning. Without them, I would not have had the drive and courage to proceed. Finally, thanks to Catherine and Larry Lawton of Cladach Publishing for putting this all together with such creativity. Here are lists of all the wonderful people who have helped.

Photographers: Chris Adams, Karen Burdick, Pat Burdick, Lisa Carlson, Bill Cassell, Carol Cassell, Dr. John Dennehy, Kirk Dorn, Chris Head, Dr. Ed Holroyd, Amber Jones, Joyce Kepto, Mike Kepto, Larry Lawton, Cathy Lyons, Eileen Maetzer, Charissa McCaslin, Kent Nelson, Marilyn Osborne, Jana Osterlund, Jeff Osterlund, Dr. Daniel Price, Brooke Roberts, Chris Roberts, Christy Roberts, Perry Roberts, Arnold Wheat, Dr. Michelle Williamson, Dr. Marc Yasoni.

Models: Kaiya Adams, Mckenna Adams, Mason Adams, Bev Bunch, Caleb Cassell, Carol Cassell, Maddy Cassell, Matt Cassell, Kevin Coffey, Kirk Dorn, Marilee Dorn, Colton Head, Ellianna Johnson, Michael Johnson, Joyce Kepto, Mike Kepto, The Kepto family, Steve and Sherrill Kautz, Matthew Lawton, Isabelle Lawton, Bob Lyons, Bobby Lyons, Megan Lyons, Kent Nelson, Jana Osterlund, Jeff Osterlund, Jessi Osterlund, Bert Perry, Laurene Perry, Shirley Ramsey, Brooke Roberts, Cade Roberts, Chris Roberts, Christy Roberts, Cole Roberts, Emory Roberts, Kurt Roberts, Perry Roberts, Breanna Slike, Ric Taylor, Marge Werske, Jeri Williams, Elin Williamson, Dr. Michelle Williamson.

ABOUT THE AUTHOR

Susan Roberts grew up in Massachusetts, one of four children. She attended Wheaton College in Illinois, received a BA in English and teaching, and MA in Interdisciplinary Studies including Christian Education and Communication. Susan met her husband, Perry, at Wheaton, where they were married and, after graduation, entered life in the military.

As a military wife, Susan was active in the post chapel programs as a board member of PWOC (Protestant Women of the Chapel). She had numerous speaking engagements with the chapel, PWOC, and Christian Women's Club, was a Bible study leader, and taught both adult and children's classes. As a mom of three, she was active with PTA, school activities, and soccer teams. At each duty station, she loved exploring interesting places with family and friends.

When Perry retired from the military, they moved to Colorado, where Susan worked twenty years with the Jefferson County School district as a school secretary. Recently retired, she and Perry have visited all fifty states and hope to visit all the National Parks. Susan enjoys wildlife sightings, especially spotting bears and watching foxes in her backyard. She loves cooking and gardening, and is an enthusiastic fan of her kids' and grandkids' soccer teams. Sue writes a bi-weekly devotional based on "God sightings" for the Arvada Covenant Church prayer line. She shares her devotions on her Facebook page at https://www.facebook.com/Susan-Perry-Roberts-961508897297583/.

CPSIA information can be obtained
at www.ICGtesting.com
Printed in the USA
FSOW04n1045051216
28138FS